Bluff & Vine
a literary review

Issue Five
Fall 2021

© 2021 by Keuka Writes.

Authors hold the rights to their individual works.
All rights reserved.

Founding Editors:
Alex Andrasik & Bethany Snyder

Cover art by Cathy Fraser.
Artwork may not be copied without permission.

ISBN: 9798755134057

Printed in the United States of America.

*Special thanks to the
Penn Yan Public Library
for their support.*

Submission guidelines at
bluffandvine.com

Contents

Whaling at Seneca Lake | James Hancock | 1
One Bad Neighbor | Nonna Shtipelman | 3
School | Ruth Anne Smyth Reagan | 6
Buffalo Bill: A Ballad | Becky Holder | 10
Cardinal Rule | Ellen Hirning Schmidt | 12
Summer Lake | Carol Mikoda | 13
Better Off | Roger A. Page | 14
A Romp | Lucas Smith | 24
Some Other Brothers | Marlana Kain | 25
Girl With Ponytail, Running | Joan Mistretta | 32
Seventy-Fourth Birthday... | Dewey Hill | 33
Fall Episodes | Jun Liu | 35
Memory of Sunrise Over Seneca Lake | Frank Hill | 38
Cooking Up History | Sally L. White | 39
Three Ladies of Keuka Lake | Adele Gardner | 43
Potting Shed | Gary Snook | 48
dark sky moon on a hook | Ron Bailey | 49
Convocation | Alex Andrasik | 50
Villanelle: Keuka | Christine Pyanoe | 68
Home | Sarah Pinneo Talley | 69
My Memories of Elmira, NY | Bard Prentiss | 71
Christmas Miracle | Carolyn Clark | 76
October Storm | Ron Bailey | 77
Gift on East Lake Rd. | Joan Mistretta | 78
Two Hundred Years and Counting | Daphne Solá | 79
The Memory of Water | Laura Dennis | 80

Looking at an Old Photograph... | Dewey Hill | 85
Road Remedy | Agnes McClear | 87
Old Friend | Gary Snook | 88
Manure Pile Muse | Carolyn Clark | 89
The Way of the Lake | Carol Mikoda | 91
The Great Roseland Indignity | John Buchholz | 92
July Sunset | Ron Bailey | 107
Creek | Linda McLean | 108
Stone Throwers | Kirk House | 110
Abandoned Barn | Gary Snook | 115
Muck | Bethany Snyder | 117
Ever Green | Carolyn Clark | 127
A Change of Diet | Carol Mikoda | 128
The Importance of Place | Laurie Weller | 129
Monica's Pies... | Karen Lee Hones | 132
If Perry City Sounds Too Grand | Daphne Solá | 136

A Note from the Editors

Five years ago, we sat at a table at Penn Yan Public Library after another fun Keuka Writes workshop and talked possibilities. We confessed to each other that we would both love to create a literary magazine, an idea that seemed so aspirational—a notion beyond the realm of reality. It hit us all of a sudden, though: what was stopping us? We didn't need anyone's permission. We could just do it. And so we did. Bluff & Vine was the result, and five years and five issues later, we're still giving ourselves permission to expand and feature ever-greater arrays of local writing talent.

This is one of our founding stories—our creation myth, if you will. It happens to be pretty much true, but that doesn't make it less of a myth—because a myth is a story with power, whether personal or universal. A myth is a story that teaches us how to tell the truth. In that way, any story has the potential to be mythic: the fondly-remembered Saturday morning cartoon that taught you what it means to be a hero; the Great American Novel that helped you cope with the absurdity or banality of real life; maybe even the short story or poem from a local literary magazine that struck you at just the right moment, delivering a much-needed insight or momentary reprieve...

Hey, anything's possible. Even if that's just another story we're telling ourselves about the power of this work, ours and that of every other poet and storyteller featured between these pages. This is how we tell ourselves the truth—by hoping to make a difference, articulating it, inviting others to share it, and then giving it to the world. To you, reader.

This is the biggest issue we've yet produced, and we are so proud to introduce you to so many new voices, as well as to welcome back some familiar friends. We're presenting you with more stories, from more perspectives, rooted in more settings from around our region than ever.

As you read through the stories and poems in this collection, pay attention to the ones that move you the most. They will be different pieces for every reader, but we're confident that each one has that potential. Fiction or memoir, prose or verse, they will take their place among the powerful tales that teach you about the world, or your community, or your family, or yourself. They will form a part of your personal mythology, alongside the TV series you love, the picture book you read to pieces as a kid, or the unpublished manuscript you may have in a drawer somewhere.

This, too, is how we tell ourselves the truth.

Sincerely,
Bethany Snyder & Alex Andrasik
Founding Editors

Whaling at Seneca Lake
poetry from James Hancock

Placid, serene, today the lake's a mild,
wordless surface, like the archaic ice
once gouging and grinding its hidden ground
for nothing, blank slate, of nothing to say,
a mute mirroring of day's sunlit sky,
of night's changeable moon-glare,
of the invisible creep of obedient stars.

Look, Bob, this lake's Ishmael's Pequod,
here, now, of Herman's breathable air,
but still today, ours, a taut skin
of apparent ice, no wind-whipped
waves, as if passion might settle for patience.
And yet, old lakes conceal their secret,
which (unpredictable) can surface again,
like a white whale's wrinkled brow
or worse, an amputee's stomping anger
harpooning his own anonymous face,
piercing by curse his mildness as mask.

But not today, this lake's all mirror,
voiceless, of the inaudible hum of balm,
pregnancy's oceanic mystery ready to erupt
in surprise, the necessary syllables and gaps
that breathe again our watery letters, the words
of depressed outrage, the peaks and troughs
of a mind (wounded) raging for adequate voice.

Once Bob, long since, we team-taught
American lit. You had the novelists,

I had the poets–and how we could lust
at the lectern, fresh, confident, masked
in our potent degrees, puffed up, entitled–
how we had learned so much, so soon!
Now, quieted, silenced as Melville once,
we must patiently await stark passion's
terrible witness to mind's emerging whiteness,
two darkening, mild-mannered professors
(once handsome almost as Billy Budd)
of balding authority, of an ignorance learned,
"a dumb blankness full of meaning" erased,
yet hoping our fire's last word to be cool
as Buddha's phenomenal, immediate smile.

—for Bob Herzog

One Bad Neighbor
fiction from Nonna Shtipelman

It was so much easier to kill your neighbor in the 1950s, at least according to the *Alfred Hitchcock* episodes we've been watching. Two with dinner every night. It gets dark early now, so there's no guilt watching the tiny screen perched on the table in front of the big window. It's too dark to see the water or the boats going by. Too dark to watch the birds settling in for the night.

September is the very best month to be here. The summer people have gone, but summer lingers. The days grow shorter, but it's still warm enough to swim, to lounge on sunbaked rocks. It's still warm enough to wear shorts and sandals, and though we always pack a few pairs of socks, we rarely need them. Fall weather is coming, often before the end of the month, but until it does, we make the most of our second summer.

Our cottage is small but perfect, just big enough for two people and one dog. It's one of six cottages in a small bay, nestled among big trees. We call it ours, even though we're renters, and once again, we're about to lose our home.

Cottages here rarely sell. They pass from one generation to the next as grandparents age out and grandchildren grow up. But three cottages here have sold in about as many years. The reason is always the same: the neighbor. What one bad neighbor can do.

No one tells us the details, but it's clear that things have never been easy. Arguments over cutting trees, over trapping muskrats for no good reason, over flying a Confederate flag. There have been calls to the police, mostly to document things should they get worse, and motion sensing cameras hung under eaves. I don't need to know the details to see the damage done. The For Sale signs say it all.

As sad as I am, I am determined to enjoy the month. It will be our last month here, after all, and I want to make the most of it. Pre-coffee paddles around the Bluff, board games on the dock, long walks along leafy trails. I will not let what's happening ruin my time here. It's not easy, but I am determined to make this a good month.

Yesterday L and the dog left for home. The yard will need mowing and there will be weeds to pull. The garden will need to be tidied up and the first fall leaves will have to be raked. I would let the yard and garden run wild, but L insists. We want to be good neighbors, after all. That means it's just me here the few days they're gone. Just me and the neighbor.

I keep the radio on for company. Last night, a report of a lost boater. With so few people on the water, you can't just assume you'll be rescued if something goes wrong. I've wanted to drag the kayak down more than a few times, but I'd be on my own and I think twice every time. There's no point in risking it.

But the neighbor still goes out, almost every day. There are life jackets on the boat, but no one ever wears one. I know this because I am a careful observer. Years ago, I had a job watching wildlife in a remote corner of southeast Alaska. I spent the summer sitting in the same spot on the same beach, scanning for movement every fifteen minutes. I still have the field journals, filled with notes and sketches.

This morning, I listen to the radio as I drink my coffee. The missing boater's skiff has been found. The missing boater has not. And now there's rough weather coming, strong winds and a small craft advisory.

I watch the neighbor walk down the dock. I could follow, suggest we join the search for the missing boater before the weather closes in. I know what the answer will be. Despite what we do on land, we always help one another on the water. I know the answer will be yes.

I also know how easy it would be to slip on a wet deck, how quickly an accident can happen, and how much less likely a happy outcome becomes when life jackets are stowed under seats. I am absolutely certain I could bring the boat home on my own.

I zip up my own life jacket and walk out the door.

School
nonfiction from Ruth Anne Smyth Reagan

Author's Note: This story occurred in my early days of going to school in Addison, New York, a small town in the southern tier of New York State, near the lower Finger Lakes.

In the autumn there is a special quality of the air, a certain blueness of the clear sky, a unique shininess of the pavement in the rain, that bring back feelings from long ago about the starting of school. From the first day I went, clutching my box of Crayolas, to this very September, as I watch my grandchildren prepare for the Grand Day, there is a feeling of excitement within me. More than at New Year's I want to make resolutions and organize my life better. I am annually full of optimism that I *will* be better, and this will be a good year.

In my mind I see the image of a small girl, for whom this is the greatest adventure of her life. I see her skipping down the street in a new plaid dress, hurrying over the sidewalks of slate and concrete. It is a long walk, nearly a mile, and it is early, too early to walk with her mother, who had to be at work in the Post Office at eight, and much too early to ride with helpful neighbors who will drive their children and others to school. She is eager to be one of the first children on the playground, and she is bursting with pride at being allowed to begin each day with the privilege of walking to school *by herself*.

Of course that child is I, six years old. I loved that walk, every inch of it, going by the big houses with stone retaining walls, by the churches, over the bridge, past the wreckage of the summer's flood, past Shelansky's candy store, and then coming in sight of the solid brick wing of the building where I attended first grade. Beside the thrill of seeing the school there was also a little panic, for my teacher was Miss Florence Malone, the Terror.

Miss Malone lived across the street from me, and in the years when we were just neighbors, she was a family friend whom everyone called Flossy. She seemed to me to be a very special friend who took me for rides in her car and brought me storybooks when I had the measles. As the teacher, "Miss Malone," she was severe, even cruel. She pinched and shook children and made them stand in the corners of the room. My greatest fear was that someday she would turn *on me*.

Yet school itself was wonderful, the way it began each day with music, and Miss Malone at the piano. There were charts that pulled down from the ceiling, and cases of books that surely contained the secrets of the world. Number work was fun. Learning to read and write was a miracle. The other children were gradually becoming my friends, although I was wary of the ones who seemed to make Miss Malone very angry. *Talking, whispering*, those seemed to be the worst sins.

The best part of school was this early time on the playground, soaring on the swings, higher, higher, the air rushing around me, *flying*! It was worth the long walk to get there before the other children. Too soon they would come, lining up, clamoring for their turn. When I had to relinquish my swing, I would stand in line to get another turn before the bell would ring to signal the starting of school.

On this particular morning I had finished a lovely turn of swinging and was dreamily standing in line when something heavy hit me on the head. Putting my hand up to feel the bump, I pulled it back covered with blood. A swing, with someone in it, had struck me; I had been standing too near the whole apparatus.

"Go to your teacher!" the children cried. Oh no, not Miss Malone! She would punish me for standing too near the swings! "Go to the school nurse!" they yelled...but I could not! She was another one of my neighbors, nice enough, but I feared that like Flossy who had turned into mean Miss Malone, the nurse would also turn into an ogre. I wanted my mother! I would go to my mother at the Post Office! And I ran as fast as I could, past the candy store, past the muddy, flood-wrecked houses by the river, across the street from the movie theatre, over to the Post Office.

The Post Office windows were closed. They were "sorting mail." No one was supposed to disturb them when they were sorting mail. Now the tears really came. I crossed the street back to the movie theatre. I put my hand to my head and felt lots more blood. Now it was beginning to hurt. What in the world was I going to do?

Down the street shuffled Old Red Barnes, looking like a pile of abandoned laundry. He had slid from his perch in front of the liquor store, and was looking for what was making such snuffling, sobbing noises. His puffy eyes blinked when he saw me weeping. "Whassamatter, lil girl?"

Never before had I heard him say a word, although I knew who he was. I was a bit afraid of him, but close up I could see his eyes were kind. I let loose, wailing about being hit by the swing, and my Mama at the Post Office, and it being closed, and the awfulness of the whole thing. He took me by the hand, led me back across the street, opened the heavy Post Office door and banged on the inner door. "Open up in there! Open up! Ther's a lil girl hurt out here!" I looked at him in awe. How brave he was! He wasn't a bit afraid of the Sorting Mail time.

Mama herself opened the door and took me in her arms. Red did not wait to be thanked, but shuffled back to the doorway of the liquor store. Mama grabbed her pocketbook and took me down the street and up the stairs to the doctor's office. He cleaned me off, stitched me up, and handed me a lollipop. Then, to my horror, Mama cheerfully sent me back to school. My heart turned to iron. Back to school? What would Miss Malone do to me? I was Late. "But I can't go back! I'm Late! The bell has rung!"

She assured me that everything would be all right. She wrote a note and sent me off. I went, but as if to an execution. Outside the first grade door I stopped. The scent of oiled floors and lunchtime oranges mingled. I could hear the squeak of blackboard chalk and the rumble of moving chairs. Out of the building, down the street I ran, past the candy store, past the movie theatre, into the Post Office, open now, and into my mother's arms. "*I couldn't* go back! It was too late! They wouldn't let me in!"

For a minute Mama was very quiet. She suspected that I was lying, but she did not scold. She hugged me, and let me play with the rubber stamps in the Post Office until noon. We had lunch together, then I went back to school, calmer now. All the other children were returning after lunch. The injury had been just a surface wound that bled a lot. I learned to keep my distance from the swings when I was not swinging myself. And I learned that my mother was surely the one to turn to when bad things happen.

This is one of my strongest childhood memories. I never forgot that gnawing fear of grownup friends whom school could turn into strangers, or the gentle concern of the town drunk, or the fear I had that Being Late was worse than Being Hurt, or the sweetness of my mother who decided that my small lie was worth overlooking sometimes. These thoughts came in handy when I myself became a mother.

Buffalo Bill: A Ballad
poetry from Becky Holder

Buffalo Bill barreled in
    the winter they were ten.
New flexible flyer, Beach Boy hair,
    he looked like young John Glenn.

The wind off Erie blew him east to a smaller, crooked lake
    and dumped him with the snow.
They were instant allies, a skinny girl with ice skates,
    blond boy with sled in tow.

They built cragged ski ramps on the hill behind her house
    and dared each other higher.
In spring they scaled a white-water gorge,
    summers, they set fires.

Bill dated her best friend, of course,
    all four high school years.
She heard both sides of every quarrel,
    and mopped up all the tears.

Best friend left shortly after graduation,
    and Bill and girl headed to a bar.
They dared each other high again
    in the backseat of his car.

Finally, in an abandoned winery,
    dim and dank with must,
the two surrendered—guiltily—
    to the musk perfume of lust.

They pledged allegiance to each other,
    spoke undying love.
But she went east and he went west
and what they'd raveled unwove.

She moved back home years later
    to a house by the lake and that hill
and sometimes she'll whisper to the wild west wind,
    "Come again from Buffalo, Bill?"

Cardinal Rule
poetry from Ellen Hirning Schmidt

All the long winter,
this loyal couple
pluffed and plump
through each epic night of warm-staying,
brave and blazing
through each marathon day of food-finding,
alight together at the feeder.
Last spring, he slipped kernels into her hungry beak and
she in turn created their cradle,
now a cup of vanilla ice cream
dolloped and mounded white in the bare forked branches.
Here her warm breast cuddled their speckled eggs,
nestled in the bush between
now leafless twigs that
scuff the still dormant sky.
My husband's gray-haired head turns to mine,
we follow the couple as they
arrive together at the feeder
this bright bold morning.

Summer Lake
poetry by Carol Mikoda

The lake and I pray deeply for each other
in this haze. Misty air hides all
but a small share of the view -- the south end,
the north have disappeared in a gauzy vapor.
I want to paddle to the edge, where fog and future
wait, past that shadowy tree on the point.

My thoughts decay to childhood, where I play
under the creaking ironing board while my mother
presses my father's shirts. The hot metal
hisses along starched cotton; steam
sighs out of the iron as she sets it down
after finishing a sleeve. Droplets gurgle
from recycled Pepsi bottle as she shakes it to dampen
the cloth. An aging celebrity croons
and jests on fuzzy AM radio.

Not staying long in that static, I return
to the sheen of grey-green waves, the shaded
blue hills like softest frayed chambray,
unravelling into the distance, sliding
down the far shore, framed by ballet
of purple martins. The waves, the birds and I,
we gauge the dew point, screen the insect swarms,
weigh the wail of a train whistle
across miles, a rooster's crowing across yards.

My devotions finished, I walk back to a world
of cell phones and junk mail, but I hold in my mind
the fogged jade of swaying water,
the fine mesh of humid air.

Better Off
nonfiction from Roger A. Page

To begin bluntly, Keuka Lake is how I overcame my alcohol addiction. I'll tell you about it.

Waking on the morning of November 10, 1984, I warily opened my eyes and stared at the ceiling. It took a couple blinks to unleash a surge of leftovers from the night before, beginning at the point where my wife, Karen, was summoned to the local State Trooper's barracks to drive me home after my arrest... my fourth arrest. Once home, she braved the darkness and briskly walked a quarter-mile down the road to retrieve my car. That's how close I came to making it home. How unlucky can a guy be, I thought at the time; but in the long run I have made peace with the opposite. Who knows what might have eventually happened to me, or others, had I made it all the way home that night? Deny or defy fate, but history suggests I was a man in dire need of a defining moment. Otherwise, when would I have stopped? I'm droning, and anyway we are not born to fathom beyond what is, or what was. Back to the story, when Karen returned to our small trailer, she toted a cold can of beer she had retrieved from my front seat and handed it over. Like a real champ I popped the top, but then, unlike any before it, I ceremoniously christened it as the last. Such a proclamation seemed worthy of monumental drama, so I stared it down, momentarily deliberating the theatrics of leaning back and draining it. But instead, totally out of character, but totally, too, out of bullets, I walked over to our kitchen sink and emptied it, thus drawing the curtain to the night of November 9, 1984. I was twenty-nine years old is all, some say just a hellraising kid, but the truth is I would not be here today, in fact would not have been here long, had I not drawn that curtain.

Now, staring at the ceiling on the morning of November 10, without further deliberation I moved from our bedroom and stood in front of our bathroom mirror. More than symbolically I wanted a last look at one of us and a lingering look at the other. I locked onto my own eyes and purposefully stood still for long moments before arriving at a decisive sigh meant to prominently raise the curtain to… well… I didn't know. How could I? Something better, I guess.

Anything.

And of all the upcoming oddities, what gamblers call an ace in the hole and magicians call a trick up their sleeve, my hopes would come to hinge upon a taped-together fishing rod and the ragged shoreline of nearby Keuka Lake. But oh, the doors they did open.

This fishing pole I mention had all the earmarks of, "Ya gotta start somewhere." Pink for one, a guide-eyelet missing out near the end, and a molded housing cracked severely enough so the reel could fall right to your feet—often. On my first outing at Keuka I had yet to discover just how poorly the faulty junction fit. I would lose count of how many times I cast the tapered half of my rod out into the lake. At its worst, there came one meltdown so decisive the whole charade unraveled simultaneously—the end of my rod soared airborne in the same motion that my reel plopped down to the ground at my feet. I stooped, picked up my reel, reassembled it, and only then could I reel in the detached section of my rod. I'm sure inebriated fishers have looked more adept. Do I really need to say how many fish I caught that day? No. Of course not. But coming home I drove past every beer joint—which, after all, was the whole point.

That night, I chased down a roll of duct tape to secure the junction of my pole, and the following morning, and each thereafter for the rest of winter, I drove to Keuka Lake minus a driver's license and drove home each night stopping only for gasoline and an occasional bag of Doritos. In time, I came to develop enviable fishing skills, while never again owning a pink fishing rod, for crime's sake. Over the years I invested thousands of dollars on everything imaginable pertaining to how to catch fish and have amassed countless memories. Now, nearly forty winters have passed.

At the time, I jokingly referred to Keuka Lake as "my sponsor," a term Friends Of Bill W, the assemblage of Alcoholics Anonymous, recognize as their most righteous ally. Each member of AA relies on a sponsor to be ready at any hour to come to their rescue. It is often the lifeline from a sponsor that saves the most fragile alcoholic and wrests them from the scrapheap of failure. I might have gladly chosen AA as a rehabilitation strategy had I no other means. Instead I trusted my wife, I trusted fishing, and I trusted Keuka Lake. My sponsors propped safety nets at every turn should I tempt a fall.

As for fishing, I was immediately as abysmal at it as I've already hinted. I had but a pocketful of lures called Rapalas - fishers know what I'm talking about - and I've already adequately revealed my rod and reel to be of yard sale caliber. But on the plus side, a friend had shown me a place on Keuka's shoreline where I could spend days, weeks, and months, tossing lures. Being laid off from my seasonal landscaping job, it turned out to be a good thing I had plenty of time. Whatever I was doing wrong on day one persisted for an awful while. Day in and day out the only way I had of knowing fish resided in the water where I cast was by witnessing other fishers occasionally hooking, fighting, and besting a trout or two. Sticking with it, it took well beyond a week for me to at last feel a subtle tick-tick-tick at my rod tip just before an intense jolt warped the entire rod into a sharp arc.

I can vividly and forever relive that celebrated occurrence.

The crystal water and morning sun, drag zipping from my shoddy reel, and my face tightening between tension and elation as whatever had struck my Rapala dove for the depths and struggled to break free.

I hadn't a clue as to how to fight a fish like this, hadn't thought this far ahead. I surmised it a good time to reel when I felt the tide turn my way. Slowly I thought to be gaining, and now my eyes strained for a glimpse of the fish. An audible gasp met the sudden flash below the surface. I doubted my chances to land this fish, I had no reason not to, but I seized the moment anyhow. I felt vibrant, sober, and better off. When my taut line rose toward the surface, the fish, like a shining missile, vaulted once, twice, three times, in rapid succession, miraculously staying hooked after each soaring aerial...

I must have taken twenty photos of that fish, a silver landlocked salmon, my first from Keuka. I landed another landlocked salmon that day, too, and returned home to a hero's welcome. Karen ogled my catch and we each marveled at the silvery brilliance of the twin salmon. Each one weighed over three pounds, far and away the largest fish I had ever caught. When I filleted them, a clumsy process at that point, the meat fascinated us, too, a translucent orange that wound up tasting not nearly as good as it looked—but give me time, I had lots to learn about cooking fish.

I had much to learn about other aspects as well.

As each successive fish hit the beach and months rolled over into years and years rolled on toward a lifetime, along the path to maturity there arose expanding overtones of an entirety in which contesting my alcohol addiction on Keuka's shoreline would be just the start. Since that first year of coming to Keuka I have somewhat melded into the landscape. I have made hundreds of friends here, and fished its waters now wall-to-wall going on forty years.

Today I am sixty-six years old and no longer lose sleep over the upcoming fishing day, but nonetheless am up and running and tooting and waving at every beer joint on my way to get to the Branchport boat launch before daybreak. As far as fish catching these days, that still matters, but in a more pedestrian way. In my age I often treasure, equal to fish, listening for the first shriek of a hovering gull or the fluttering whup-whup-whup of a zooming mallard, and in rare instances over Keuka there are now bald eagles to keep an eye out for, too. Sometimes, and I doubt I've ever said this aloud to anyone, I sit in my fishing boat without a line out. I shut my eyes and listen for whatever is at hand. Generally at daybreak the water is eerily still, and from a distance, I am posed as a silhouette perched motionless upon what might as well appear as a sheet of glass. The only sound once I cut my 40-horse after propelling out here is an inconspicuous metallic clank from my thermos, and the cool air erupts with the friendly smell of strong black coffee, the kind where you lean close and intentionally inhale for all you're worth. I am closer to the west shore. There is a certain area of water over here where I like to start off fishing, but I would probably start here anyhow; the eastern horizon on Keuka Lake at sunrise is stunning, and this affords the optimal view. I have practiced being positioned in time to watch each layer. The last star fading, the steel gray sky acquiescing to a brightening cobalt horizon that is short-lived, soon devoured by a glowering crimson impetus like fire to ice. The intensity smolders, warming an unspoken communion shared by the early morning crowd from wherever they are watching, all of us anticipating a grand finale, the upcoming likeness of bursting flames.

On mornings like these I will have not yet thought much about fishing, despite it being the principal reason I am here. Fishing is so deep-seated by now there isn't much to think about. But a sunrise, that's different. One must never grow complacent about sunrises. Always a sunrise is cause for, first, quiet celebration, and then unhurried deliberation. In comparison, fishing is just as often a whim, so I begin these mornings with fishing rods stored, trolling motor silent, and boxes of lures and accessories momentarily unattended.

First, there is a Keuka sunrise coming.

&

If I seem overly enthused by this sunrise business, there is another thing I need to tell you; it will explain my well-founded reason why another day, simply by coming, earns such limelight.

Cancer.

Yeah. Can you believe it? I had no sooner semi-retired from my lifelong livelihood of operating a landscaping business, all sorts of time now for Keuka Lake and fishing, deer hunting, riding a hot run of nationally published magazine articles in outdoor magazines, full-speed-ahead authoring self-published books, and then one evening in mid-May 2017, I mentioned to Karen about a slight earache that had begun gnawing. A week later she purchased a heating pad for me to prop beneath my ear so I could sleep. A few days later is when I discovered the swollen lymph node in my neck.

For anyone who has not been there, and how I hope you never are, you cannot imagine the gripping horror that envelops you the instant you learn you are going to be fighting cancer. No matter how conscientiously or delicately the diagnosis is conveyed, your heart plummets, your face locks in fear, you cannot speak, and your next breath, probably the next several, will come in gasps.

Doc Sussman, an ENT specialist, guided his endoscope up my nostril, and it took only seconds for him to see what he needed to. He removed the scope, slid his chair back, and said to me, "I'm afraid I have to lower the boom a bit, here," and everything good to say about Keuka Lake, fishing, writing, and anything else that had once happily steered my life, screeched to a halt. My diagnosis was HPV virus—specifically carcinoma at the base of the tongue and the adjacent lymph node mentioned earlier.

I could go on and on - heck, I authored an entire book about it. The fight was awful, thirty-three radiation jolts to the neck area, three massive chemotherapy sessions, salivary glands and taste buds temporarily destroyed, my throat rendered dysfunctional, meaning I fed for months through a feeding tube. My voice fell mute for six full weeks, and at its lowest point depression took hold for longer than I like to admit. An awful fight.

That should be enough said about that part of it, just please don't lose sight that what I am still talking about are sunrises, and why for some of us they have become daily miracles.

I saw a lot of bravery in the Corning Cancer Center that winter, and still do each time I visit for routine checkups. I'm on the other side now, where each day is a gift. But while I was there daily, among the many ordinary people that had turned courageous by demand, there is one I can count on to bring this story full circle.

Undergoing cancer treatments, my scheduled time for radiation each weekday morning was 10:30, so each day I would arrive close to 10:15. One morning I sat in the lobby waiting my turn when acquaintances of mine, Woody and his lifelong companion, Susan, entered. Woody was fighting a cancer far more aggressive and severe than mine, but remained determined to stay gallant. They smiled to see me there and came and sat down. Woody and Susan live nearby, so we were at least casual friends before this, but had naturally developed a tighter rapport due to our common circumstances. That morning, out of the blue, Woody informed me, "Got a little trip planned for me and you next summer." He then elaborated that we would be gearing up for a fishing trip, and not just an afternoon out on Keuka, either; no, Woody was talking two to three days and traveling out of state to boot. He was happy to know I could be relied upon to be ready to go at the drop of a hat.

What I haven't said yet is that Woody was an accomplished professional at fishing. He zoomed about the entire northeast all summer long from lake to lake. I paled by comparison. Unfortunately, though, as I hinted, our cancers weren't remotely in the same ballpark, either. Woody's cancer attacked his liver and pancreas. Mine was the HPV virus as I described. My prognosis projected the worst upcoming months of my life; Woody's prognosis projected… well… Woody's prognosis projected we shouldn't be planning a fishing trip.

As expected, instead of a fishing trip the following summer, I attended a springtime Celebration Of Life to honor Woody. The room teemed with people I had never met, but not once did I feel like a stranger. The more I meandered about the gathering, chatting it up with Woody's buddies, the more I wished to have known him better. I think, though, mine was the most poignant story to share. Catering to melancholy smiles I told them all about two old fishers sitting in the lobby of the local cancer center, one of them here today for chemo, the other for radiation, but in the meantime planning a… a… a *fishing* trip?

I suppose without being at the cancer center that morning to hear, in person, Woody's proposal, one might not absorb its fullest impact. Only if you were sitting right there next to Woody and Susan to hear it, to feel it, and to look directly into their eyes, where all hope should be gone, could you appraise the moment as so torturously real it rips your heart through your chest. Only then could you entirely grasp what gigantic, optimistic strength we can carry forth with us each day we are granted.

We are back on Keuka, now, the sunrise leaving on its wing a warming regal purple horizon. A purring breeze ripples the surface. The gift of a new day unwrapped, new promises, new chances; it's time to get fishing.

I once devoted an entire book to fishing, but knew I could have written more… and then more. Fishing is boundless to those who see it that way—the type who rarely fret much about fish. I perhaps shouldn't lament so poetically as to imply that catching them never matters; sometimes it does. But generally a day fishing can be measured simply because of itself. And as long as I'm invited here to shine light upon Keuka Lake, the same can be said for her.

In the introduction of that book I reiterated an age-old enigma, "Why do you fish?" I first encountered the seemingly elementary question in a book titled *The Compleat Angler*, written by Izaak Walton centuries ago in 1653, lest you think it's such an easy question. I don't have to go back and read my own version where I posed the question from the eyes of a fictional old-timer finishing up a cup of coffee before heading out for the day. My intent from the get-go was to breathe life into that old-timer, and I since have, but growing into my own prophetic pages was not as easy as I had planned, given that little detour directly through the pit of hell, but here I am. These days, out in the driveway under the stars ahead of dawn, I give the tie-downs a quick once-over and check the trailer lights, ready for the trip to Keuka to further pursue the nagging question, "Why Do You Fish?" I know I'm not fooling you one lousy bit by adding weight to the question, and I suspected right from the start the most truthful answer would not be philosophical, complex, or even interesting. For fun, knowing I would never dare write it this way, I jokingly brushed aside all dramatizing and answered it right out loud… "Who cares?" And then I laughed for minutes and even hours afterward.

My journey in hand with my proven sponsor, Keuka Lake, is, I guess, winding down, might as well say it out loud. I still hope to have some good years left, though; I surely have a nice boat for it, and my perspective stays eager and strong, fortified by the sobriety I found here, and the renewed chances I have been granted to continue seeking all there is to find here.

I love this lake.

There is no finer place where I would rather come clean and fully address the enigma of why I fish. And I answer it especially thinking of addicts trying to find a new and better way, I answer on behalf of my friend Woody and anyone else fighting cancer, and even as my heart breaks I reach to the very ends of my soul and pull for them to see new sunrises.

There should be no further need to spell it out. The answer to why I fish is because the sun came up for me again today. And it shone on me out here amid bluish glistening sparkles and waves of memories that carry all the way back to a pink fishing pole, a silver flash, and a kept promise that I would spend my lifetime better off for having come here.

A Romp
poetry from Lucas Smith

Every now and then a smell of dirt or
A cold damp in my sock, the loosening of
Mud underneath my boot gives me a hunger;
A familiar madness demands to feast
On the smell of woodsmoke, the ache in my legs
And the taste of dust as windows are opened
To receive the sunlight that seeps through my shirt.
Drunk of the last fermented days of winter,
Dizzy from the sudden openness of sky,
The plunge of spring is a joyful vertigo.

Some Other Brothers
fiction from Marlana Kain

When the moon is high in the sky, and perfect and round and bright, it lays a shiny white path across the lake right to our cottage. I know it means we're special.

Mom cleared the dinner plates, while Papou watched Jeopardy and then came out to sit on the screened porch. His old hands, with the blue veins popping out like a road map, held on to the arms of the chair. He always sat in that rickety old chair. Mom told me he brought it from his old house on Sawyer Street. It reminded him of Yiayia and when they were young. Andrew and Zoe were playing giant checkers on the picnic table. Zoe jumped. "King me!"

Papou rocked and sang. I think he was trying to capture my attention away from the checkers game.

"Good evening friends,

we recommend

Blue Plate Number Two.

Our food is best in the whole wide west.

What can we do for you?"

In the old days, Papou owned the Blue Bird restaurant, next to the bus station in the city, and he knew a lot of things. He sipped ginger ale from my favorite tall glass, the one with the frost and green leaves on it. Then he jiggled the ice around and put it back down on the stool. I watched him open his brown plastic pouch and scoop out some tobacco with his pipe, packing it in with his thumb. Soon the whole porch smelled like warm vanilla.

"Two Pockets, come sit." He patted the cot next to his chair with his left hand, while he held the pipe in his right. I plopped down, crossed my legs and watched the swirl of smoke.

Papou called me Two Pockets because he teased that I always had my hands in my pockets. I kept stuff in there, like the tie dye ball from the gum ball machine at the barber shop, extra ride tickets, or my favorite race car from Monopoly.

He looked out at the smooth water. "The Seneca knew when the moon was full, there would be the most fish in the lake." Papou knew things like that.

"I think those guys who fish in front of the Baileys' cottage know too. Maybe we should go out on the dock early tomorrow?"

I remembered early this morning when the sun peeked over the hills and the sky was bright orange. I was awake, and I saw an old Whaler zoom across the lake from my window. A fisherman cast a line near our dock. The bass were already jumping here and there. I could hear the little splashes, and I remembered hearing the swish of the cast line and then the click, click, click of the reel.

Even though I was busy, busy, busy all day pulling seaweed, popping wheelies on the Nicholas tube, swinging on the rope swing, I never got too tired. I had so many things swirling around in my head. Sometimes when I couldn't sleep, I had to get up and walk around the cottage. Mom worried, "Teddy, are you OK?" Mom and dad slept in the first-floor bedroom next to the family room, and mom always heard everything. She even knew when I snuck in the kitchen to get one of those Little Debbie coffee cakes out of the red breadbox with the Dutch girl sticker. Other times, I just cuddled under my covers, looked out the window, and listened to the tick tock of the clock next to my bed. I liked the mornings when the water was calm, and I could hear the cardinals sing, "Cheer-cheer-cheer-purty-purty-purty."

"Let's do that!" Papou said. "Why don't you get that big silver flashlight, wet the ground and dig up some night crawlers? Those shiny lures don't fool these fish anymore."

We'd played water dodgeball earlier, like we did on most days when it was really hot and sunny. I got a little sunburn on my nose. Papou touched it with his thumb.

We only ever played dodgeball on the right side of the dock, never on the crab side where Zoe once got a bloodsucker stuck on her leg. Mrs. Bartholomey, two cottages down—who had worms in milk cartons inside her fridge—was fishing at the end of her dock. She came over and pulled it off with a rake. Mrs. B had little holes in her Keds to make room for the bunions that popped out of her feet. Sometimes she came by to have a gin and tonic with mom and dad. She'd tell stories about her Uncle Donald or one of her bad brothers. She knew a lot about blood suckers and bad people.

"We'll be putting those fishing poles away before you know it, Teddy." Then Papou asked, even though I think he knew the answer, "Soon you'll be starting fifth grade?" A puff, puff, puff of his pipe. More vanilla.

"Yep, I get a hall locker instead of a cubby this year. Mom bought me a lock, and I already memorized the combination. 12-18-89."

Summer was almost over. We'd be closing up the cottage and going home soon. Mom would take us to get #2 pencils, black speckled notebooks and a new backpack for the first day of school. The corn along West Lake Road was already taller than me, and it tasted almost as sweet as the 'lopes from the roadside stand. Andrew and I still had time with no homework to shuck it before Sunday dinner.

"I'm going out to make the fire if anyone wants to help."

I walked out to the lakefront. It was so quiet. The end of summer made me sad. It wasn't like July when all the cousins were here. Spero would run down the dock and cannonball into the lake, and we'd all play freeze tag on Uncle Peter's property. When the cousins were here, we'd have a big pile of Sunday pancakes with real maple syrup from Uncle Sonny's farm. Now there were more crickets than cousins and hardly ever any boats pulling skiers. Jacky from next door already went home, so we couldn't even play bloody knuckles on her porch. Sometimes I heard a hunter's shot in the morning from the hills. It made a giant echo. But it was a sound I didn't like at all.

Andrew came out, threw me my balled up Go Navy sweatshirt, and I zipped it right up because the air was cooler now too. It was like someone held their breath at the top of Bristol Mountain and let it out slowly, mixing their cold air with the leftover warm air. Mom told me when she rolled the toter up Sunday night, it looked like a big cloud hung in the yard, and she thought she saw a fisher run across the driveway. Mrs. Bailey had told her she saw a black bear across the road the other night. I was afraid it might get mom, or that a mean weasel might pop out of the woods and chase her down. I'll take up the trash next time. I'll ask Andrew to come with me.

A few fireflies lit up, and the stars sparkled so bright right above our lake. A bat swooped down low near the trees. Andrew and I skipped stones and then started on the bonfire.

"Teddy, get some twigs and I'll get the newspaper."

"OK. I saw marshmallows in the kitchen. See if Zoe wants to come out!"

Andrew took the steps a couple at a time and let the screen door slam behind him. I knew he would take the long way around the living room to stay away from the scary closet. We knew there was a ghost in that old closet under the stairs. So, I was careful to never, ever open that creaky door, even though I sort of wanted to. Once, Andrew opened it on a dare when the cousins were here. I saw some rain boots, a can of paint and an old vacuum cleaner. But I tried not to look too hard. I also remember it smelled like the attic at Thea Nounou's house when I crawled up there to help bring down her

Christmas decorations. Mostly, we never touched that old door.

I followed the sidewalk around the window side of the cottage. I saw dad inside reading the paper with his legs crossed on the ottoman. Papou was in the rocking chair next to the TV, laughing. Papou watched *Seinfeld* and still laughed like he'd heard the jokes for the first time. I like watching a show over and over too. I like when I already know the ending.

I pulled three good logs from the woodpile under the garage. Through the kitchen window, I saw Zoe and mom putting the dishes away. They were laughing too. They were always laughing about something. I laughed a lot too but not as much as I did in second grade.

I carried the wood out front and made a standing up triangle with the logs in the firepit. Then I slid down the ditch between our cottage and the Baileys' and picked up a few twigs. On the way down, I scraped my leg on that prickly bush with the little berries. I think I just missed touching a poison ivy leaf on my way back up. I counted three leaves and made sure to stay away. I poked the kindling through the triangle of logs, then grabbed the old rake leaning on the house to drag up some dried-up seaweed from above the shore. I loved making the fire and I was good at it.

Andrew came out and put down the bag of marshmallows and a couple metal skewers on the old step under the crooked tree. I love our handprints on that step—Andrew's, Zoe's and mine. I remember when Mom mixed up some concrete from Smith's Hardware, and spread a layer of it on the crumbly step like she was frosting a birthday cake. Then we took turns pressing our hands in it. Mom carved in the date with the thinnest edge of a skipping stone, so we would always remember when we were little. If there was a ton of snow in the winter, the water might be too high. Or if the summer was really hot and the water was low, dad had to add another piece of dock, so the boat prop didn't scrape the bottom of the lake. But the step with the handprints was always right there under that crooked old tree no matter what.

Zoe came out, and we set up the chairs around the cottage side of the firepit because the flag on the dock was blowing toward the lake. If you sat on the lake side, smoke might get in your eyes. Andrew and I crumbled up the newspaper and stuck it in the spaces between the logs.

Dad walked down the stairs with a pack of matches, struck one and slowly handed it to me with his hand cupping the flame. I tossed the burning match into the pile of wood and old comics. It caught fire and quickly burned out. Dad showed Andrew how to light a match and let him try. He touched the flame to the crumbled newspaper. Then I had a turn again.

"Be careful, Teddy!" Dad didn't know I already tried it once with Papou's matches from the tobacco store, when I was digging for night crawlers behind the old garage. Mom probably knew.

Andrew sat on the green and white folding chair, and Zoe was on the step measuring her hand on each of the prints. I stuck a marshmallow on the end of a perfect long twig I found yesterday. I had it saved under the steps next to the Styrofoam cup with my secret crab, the one I didn't want anyone to use as bait.

I squatted close to the heat and pushed the marshmallow into the hottest part of the fire. Then pulling it out, I watched it light up so bright, the flame hissing and burning the sweet to black. My sunburn stung a little, and I blew out the flame. Sliding off the burnt shell of the marshmallow in one piece, I popped it in my mouth. Then I slid off the pillow inside and put it right on my tongue. The soft surprise inside was the best part.

Andrew toasted his marshmallow slowly on one of the metal skewers we used for souvlaki. When he moved a little to get away from the tiny pieces of paper that floated out into the night, his marshmallow caught fire.

"Shoot!" He blew it out, pulled it off, and tossed it into the fire to start again.

Andrew turned his skewer slowly. His face looked like the face he makes when he's playing Skee-Ball. He concentrates on rolling the ball to bump it at that perfect place on the side rail, like he does, so it almost always goes right in the center circle. Andrew was really good at Skee-Ball and mostly everything. His marshmallow was caramel colored all over. He pulled it off, ate it, and toasted another one for Zoe.

Beasley, the cuddly dog next door, barked, and some waves rolled over the shale. On the porch, the windchimes jingled and some crickets chirped. But mostly it was pretty quiet and we all just watched the fire. I saw a light go on in one of the upstairs bedrooms. Papou must be getting ready for bed. It reminded me and, in a minute, I'd go dig up some nightcrawlers.

I love our bonfire nights; collecting things to put in the pile, the quick bright light and slow burn of the fire, the crackle of the wood and the pop, pop, pop of little stones. I love the smells and sounds of summer, and I love how we all just sit around roasting marshmallows and telling stories, and no one has anywhere else they have to be.

I thought about the first day of school and lining up at the bus stop in the Harpers' driveway in a new pair of Chuck Taylors. I'll get the coolest pair. I will be line leader this year, and I'll raise my hand in class. I will watch out for Zoe since Andrew will be in middle school. This year will be different. I'll do all my homework and try my hardest to wait my turn. The soccer coach will pick me to be captain, just like Andrew. I just know it. Mom and dad watched us from behind the porch screen. It was almost bedtime. I hope I can get to sleep.

Girl With Ponytail, Running
poetry from Joan Mistretta

Around here the back country roads
  need a lot of careful driving.
Our four-lanes are not clogged with traffic
  and have been made pretty straight and flat.
But the side roads can go right up, just
  a few degrees off vertical
Or worse, straight down, with tricky
  turns.
So, eyes on the road, pray for the brakes

But what is that in the corner
  of my eye?
A two-legged deer tossing its head
  defiantly?
A hopping hare just over the
  crest of the next hill?
A patriot with a flag, waving it
  with the perfect rhythm of a message drum?
A yearling racehorse learning to
  run ahead of the whip?

Too late, I'm past it now.
I'll never know.

Seventy-Fourth Birthday
Top of the Lake Restaurant
Keuka Lake 2020
poetry from Dewey Hill

Sliding a serrated knife
to slice my birthday Delmonico,
blending the tastes
of red beef juices
with mellow mold
of blue cheese,

So what if the doctors now say,
"Eat no Salt!"
And
"Drink no alcohol!"

I have smoky grilled steak
and a chilled glass of Beck's NA
with which to pretend youth.

Through the picture window
The long-winged, white gulls disappear
and,
silently,
in slips the night's black waters.

Close clusters of cottage lights
from across the lake
scatter across the picture window glass,
and mix with
almost

imperceptibly reflected

bar lights.
The old woman at the next table says,
"You look good
for seventy-four."

And then later,
after recounting a crippling chronicle
of her last three strokes,
she tells me she has a wrinkled retina.

"I don't see things so good anymore."

"Yeah," I answer, "Me neither."

Fall Episodes
poetry from Jun Liu

1. The giver

I forgive summer for leaving
The rainbow attached to its sleeves
Spilled the pot of gold
All over our home
The hills get their share
The lakes get their share
Even the stars get their share
To shine through winter
Nature has a way to spread wealth
Among all of us
And make everyone equally happy
It is the most wise and skilled giver

2. The grace

They say that what you see in others
Reveals the truth of yourself
You must believe it
When the luminous hills
Reflect your smile

They say every loss is repaid
With a gain in time
You must trust it

When autumn sun pats on your shoulder
Like a loving grandparent

They say each effort with a worthy purpose
Leads closer to your reward
You must savor it
When honeybees brush
Eyelashes of the asters

They say it's never too late
To start a new story
You must read it
When golden needles lie on ground
Awaiting silvery threads

They say all hardships shall pass
And tenderness germinates anew
In every corner
A broken shell found in the garden
Must remind you
The time when robust robins
Lay baby blue eggs

3. The marked calendar

October is coming
The last fluttering of hummingbirds is passing
Red leaves are showing
The weathered tree limbs are spreading
—We add more layers to resist
They let go brilliance to persist

November is coming
The forgetful wind is stirring
The black earth has been collecting
The fallen season is transforming
—The great law overrules the smaller ones
And fever gives in to solitude

December is coming
The determination to convert darkness is budding
The marks on the calendar are creeping
Days without names retreating
—Time does not fly
When we wait impatiently
For the next feast

4. The home

The hills glow like horizon preceding sunrise
Before which is the rise of
Goldenrod matches and sumac horn candles
Above which sugar maple holds torches
And Virginian flame creeps up banks
Soothing which are the
White, blue and purple asters
Of the wood, New York and New England names
Gazing the sky and lifting the fields

The solemn pines, firs and spruces
Pin down the flying gown
Of the radiant goddess
Whose affair with the Earth
Is no longer secret

Our lakes, streams and waterfalls
Are tie-dyed
The ripples, bubbles and splashes collage
The mist, droplets and crystals rise and rise
To tinkle on the glossy sunlight
To expand the full spectrum sunset

The evening air extends
Star trails reaching
In fragrance of saturated grapes
And drying medicine
To say good work
And good night.

Memory of Sunrise Over Seneca Lake (a series of haiku)
poetry from Frank Hill

Ring-billed gulls play king
of the pilings. Pink clouds bathe
the reflective waves.

Quilted red flannel
smelling of campfire smoke warms
me as I warm you.

We celebrate our
one year anniversary—
a soft sunrise kiss.

The gulls' piercing cries
usher in another year
of quiet reflection.

Cooking Up History
memoir from Sally L. White

History was never my favorite subject. There's a redundancy in learning the kings of England, for example, that fails to intrigue. When we're young it makes sense that we have little to do with history—it must be something we grow toward as we accumulate more of it. This is especially true of family histories and genealogy, which seem to be practiced primarily by those of us who are aging.

When we do come around to looking into our personal history, we find that it traces the contributions of the male side with precision, while female ancestors tend to fade or disappear altogether. I suspect that this happens because, historically speaking, the main thing most women have done with their lives was nourishing their families—socially, emotionally, spiritually, and physically. Traditionally, the lifework of women has gone unrecorded.

Sometimes there is more. A few old letters, perhaps. In my case, a handful of old recipes also survives. In my grandmother's unique script is the only record we have of how she nourished—and entertained—her family. Recipes in themselves aren't much to go on; my sister reminds me how we all collect recipes, many of which go unused. But these are recipes Grandma took the trouble to record—not just clipped out of a magazine or newspaper, but copied over by hand to pass on to her oldest daughter, and later her oldest granddaughter. Looking at Grandma's handwriting gives me new appreciation of the crispy old recipes in my own mother's hand, and new commitment to saving them for her grandchildren in turn.

Still, validation is necessary, as with all historical materials. When my mother was the age I've now reached, we sat sifting through these old recipes. I learned more about my grandmother—and thus my mother's childhood—than I had in the decades since Grandma's death. I learned that the house she ran was the house where all the children in the neighborhood gathered—a place that was warm and welcoming. Mom remembers a childhood of taffy pulls and popcorn balls, treats made for fun with family and friends. We attempted taffy once, but the results were dismal. Mom remembers homemade hot cocoa for kids home from sledding, and she recreated that memory (albeit with Nestlé's Quik) for our childhood. These recipes have become memories that are, in individual human terms, as permanent as anything can be.

Don't expect hand-holding here. A certain foundation is expected. In fact, you'll be pretty much on your own. Some recipes consist only of lists of ingredients. These recipes, passed from mothers to daughters for who knows how long, assume that you already know what to do with dumplings, or what temperature you will need to bake muffins. Now, of course, you need only turn to the Internet for detailed instructions on all sorts of culinary delights.

The frays and splatters that show even on the photocopies validate these recipes. As I look through them I find that taffy and those popcorn balls, recorded for posterity, as well as the cakes and cookies of daily desserts, the marmalade and mincemeat of occasional treats. Where are the everyday meals, the daily nourishment that grew another generation?

In fact, few women turn to recipes for the meals they make every day. The improvisations that became routine are formulas of flexible composition, passed down but rarely written down. A maternal legacy. Who would bother to write down instructions for pot roast or chicken and dumplings? Mom did, because when I was on my own for the first time and learning to cook, those were the very instructions I asked for, the information I needed to feel at home far from home.

So I pressed her about the day-to-day meals, the events that made up the background of her young life. And there, in the details, was a true history of how my grandparents lived—more revealing than the documented family record. A favorite of mom's, homemade chocolate pudding with whipped cream, testified to the presence of a family cow, as did homemade ice cream, plain vanilla or chocolate only. Egg salad and lemonade made summer lunches; chicken (boiled first, then fried to brown), served with biscuit and gravy, a Sunday dinner after church.

Mom remembers roast pork so juicy and tender it can't be duplicated with today's supermarket cuts. As a child, she was sent to the store with ten or fifteen cents for a pound of hamburger, then sent to bed without supper because she refused to eat the New York-style "chili" Grandma made from it—documenting Depression economics and old-fashioned family discipline at a stroke. Potato puffs with creamed salmon (canned in those days)—a time-consuming recipe that did get written down—were served only for company. Later they became the most requested birthday dinner of my own childhood. Only in adulthood did I discover Mexican or Asian food, with enthusiasm!

I think it's wonderful that in the future more kids will know their grandmothers better—Granny was a nuclear physicist or best-selling author. They'll be able to point to hard physical (and digital) evidence of who Granny was and how she spent her life. But something will be lost too. For most of my generation and all the generations before, we are the hard physical evidence of their lifework. The fact that we are alive and healthy is the proof that we were nourished—often the only testimonial we have of who our female ancestors were and how they lived.

We may forget the sights and sounds of childhood, but smells and tastes can take us immediately home. Grandma died when I was six, and I can't claim to remember much about her. But I remember the taste of her homemade vegetable beef soup (also not written down) even though I haven't tasted beef in decades. The visceral senses, perhaps because we don't often consciously attend them, have a power that is deep and lasting. Psychologists tell us that smell, recorded in the subconscious, may have a role in the experiences we call dejá vu. Not already seen, perhaps, but already smelled. It's possible, when our bodies become frail and our minds are failing, that a dimly remembered taste will still be there to trigger a host of memories. It's possible that the key to those memories is there in the recipes.

Three Ladies of Keuka Lake
poetry from Adele Gardner

Three kayaks on Keuka Lake—green, yellow, and white—
Carry Mom, my sister, and me
Three Gardner women returned, not without difficulties,
Through a long voyage
From Virginia back to the homeplace, Keuka Lake,
The one place on earth we belong.
To get here, the three of us brave all odds and dangers—
Broken-down cars, strokes, illness, death—
To reunite each year
In a place whose beauty speaks to the soul

This year, just the three of us:
Lake women intent on adventure,
Laughing and sharing memories,
Kayaking all three together almost every day

This evening we soar
Across green-blue evening waves,
Through cottage reflections,
While our lively talk revives the past
As we glide past motorboat revelers

A white butterfly, flickering above little blue-gray waves,
Moves so swiftly, bobbing in air like surf.
A seagull floats, moved along by waves.
Stones ripple on the lake bottom, visible in sunlit stripes through
    shadowy waves.
Four kayaks—blue, red, yellow, white—pass ours,
Another fleet of plastic voyagers

On a swifter journey, while we point out places
We've known across the lake
And discuss the past, not noticing how waves push us past our cottage,
Life passing swiftly while we enjoy memories

In the beauty of this lake, the past comes alive
For all to see—the grandeur of a loving heart and intelligent mind,
Dad's union with Mom one of the most precious and rare
    moments in our history,
A love and harmony so few get to enjoy:
This truth vividly brought home throughout our lives
As they joined voices in harmony in evening's gold,
Singing together before suppertime,
Before Dad fired up those pillow-coals to make steak on the grill,
And Mom pulled her cherry pie from the oven,
And we ran down the hill to the lake
For one last swim in the golden afternoon,
My favorite time of day—
When laughing Daddy came home
From his Keuka College office where Mom brought me to visit
    during the day,
And our happy family's life was complete

Now, as we slide leisurely through water and memories,
Mom speaks of attending Keuka College in the 1960s,
An all-girls' college back then, brave and true:
Her favorite final the one in canoeing.
She loved the annual May Day canoe race for fun, laughs,
But they took it seriously:
A crew of young Amazons sculling a dark green war canoe.
Her class won each year, despite the younger class having the
    bent canoe,
The one that tilted to the left, needing stronger rowers there.
The contest pitted freshmen against sophomores, juniors
    against seniors,
With the finalists dueling to the finish line at Point Neamo.
This short racecourse had the shore on their left,
Bluff Point to the rear, Penn Yan ahead.
Mom's crew's timing had to be precise
As they waited, lined up between yellow and blue cottages

For a flying start by their coxswain's stopwatch:
Dip your oars early, or you'll lose!
But don't cross the starting line early, or you're out!

In the bow, the first student rowed singly;
Next came four pairs, each woman with one paddle,
Their outer knees down, out of way of the oars.
They kneeled on the bottom of the canoe,
Cushioned only by a damp folded towel on its wooden ribs.
No seat, just a dowel at the rump for balance.
In the center, two inner knees stood upright, forming the shape
   of a chair,
Two thighs parallel with the bottom of the canoe,
Each inner leg pressed against her neighbor's
For balance, stability, and leverage,
Giving greater purchase and paddle-strength in the water:
Powerful together—a great push—
All moving in rhythm.
The lone coxswain in the stern called by megaphone to guide them:
"Left pull" and "Stroke, stroke, stroke," always in rhythm,
As they stroked, then feathered—
Stroke, feather
As they row, row, rowed to the finish line

Mom, victorious in each year she attended,
Now guides our efforts as three kayaks paddle together
Into the evening sun,
Gold crossing into the silken mysteries of night:
This twilight one of the times Between,
When the gates to other worlds open

Turning for home, we slip into silence
As the sunset builds sky castles,
A sight so incredible
We hold our breaths
As pink streaks one side of the sky
Out from a concentrated pillar
Like a burning city of old

The far shore looks mountainous with adventure:
Huge masses of clouds pink and violet, white and slate-blue,
So mammoth that a dragon might hide there
While I tilt my lance
Amid spears of molten gold

Such a shining flurry, awesome display
As the gates open and we see the fiery grandeur
Of a ruined palace, still flaming—
We might be able to save it with lake magic if we concentrate
    all our power:
But how do we know it isn't a bastion of evil, too dangerous to save,
Like the House of Usher in Poe's tale,
Or a place that entraps like Tennyson's Palace of Art,
All that beauty concentrated in one place,
Hoarded by the solitary, beauty-loving recluse
Who abandons life and humanity
Till the soul burns for that sin:
Art unlived, unshared

But here in this lake where the past comes alive,
Good Keuka carries us gently, even when we are still—
Taking me out of my solitude, my loneliness, grief large or small,
To the hush, hush, hush of the boats
As the burning city flees behind us
And we drift from one wonder to the next
In quiet, perfect joy:
To paraphrase Dad's final letter,
Love is alive!
My skin tingles as my heart brings out a favorite song:
"God Is Alive, Magic Is Afoot" by Buffy Sainte-Marie (and
    Leonard Cohen)
(Go listen, please—your body still,
Your eyes and heart focused on a lake scene)

Then a perfect sliver of crescent moon like a diadem
Emerges on the lovely blue sky
And over the forested hills and farms on the opposite shore
Horizontal stripes of orange and white,

With feathery lines spreading straight out, fanning overhead
Like a hint of transparent rainbow:
A beautiful sunset so majestic
We're struck by awe

Throughout the magnificent show,
All three kayaks drift—a single paddle here, there,
Just enough motion
To stay together while we watch in silent communion:
We paddle, then float and look,
Paddle, then float
And look
All the way home

—for M. & M.

Potting Shed
poetry from Gary Snook

The potting shed
Has a shoved out wall
And sagging windows
Too long without glass
The workbench shows traces
Of penciled reminders
The floor is red
With bits of baked clay
Scoop up some dirt
Rub your hands together
Is that imagination
Or the smell of old peat
A lingering reminder
Of a time now past
When seedlings grew
On warm spring days

dark sky moon on a hook
—coyote song
poetry from Ron Bailey

across elk creek they prowl the edge,
hill rises behind
fallen pines, chunks of limestone
the size of buffalo

young coyotes
some with richer voice
fill valley with howl
songs that shiver up fading daylight
up my ribs
up the last gasps of thursday dusk

sun has just bruised
itself on horizon edge
bleeds into clouds—

i can see your yellow eyes in the water
deer bolt to higher ground
opossum and coons to safer branches
and i to shelter listen for your
sacred chant wrap around trees

my feet scratch up the hill
stones and dirt rattle behind

Convocation
fiction from Alex Andrasik

The Convocation is a single moment and it is a thousand ages. It is always happening, but sometimes, it's happening a little bit more. More is now.

We take turns on hosting duties. It is at once a very *civilized* thing to do, and only natural—as in "of nature," where cycles rule, where the law is change. It's my turn, and I have come to the place where I am the most myself, to wait and welcome.

A woman in off-white and gold is the first to arrive, and though she has changed subtly since our last gathering, I know her. Often the punctual one, though it's not that I recognize. It's not the obvious high quality of the cream pantsuit, nor the travel cup exuding steam inflected with cinnamon. It's not only those features, though together they contribute to my sense of her as herself, as more than *herself*—as the vast, slow slosh of *knowing* behind and above and within this form before me.

"I hate how *dreary* this part always is," she says.

And she's right, though I don't share her distaste. I have always appreciated the dynamic, deadly flow, the grey sky tinged with yellow that dances before the violence. *This* is not quite *that*, though. The Convocation is every moment, and none. So much *something* piled on top of *nothing* has a foggy effect. We can still see for miles—though it's not so much seeing, as *being*—but the prospect is soupy, the shapes of water and shore indistinct.

Before I can respond with more than an indulgent smile, there's a derisive snort, and another arrives. I turn and find a tall, middle-aged man striding into the clearing around us. He's long and lean, and though his clothes have a look of quality about them as well, his choices are more rugged. Slightly. He's still wearing a button-down shirt, but the sleeves are rolled up to reveal tanned forearms, and his jeans look thick, ready for a hike. "It wouldn't be a Convocation without a snide remark from you," he fires at the other woman.

"Oh, shut up and give us a kiss," she fires back, opening her arms, and he crosses to her, holds her elbows lightly, and they peck each other on each cheek. These two are always sniping, but they're more alike than almost any of the rest of us.

I widen my smile to include them both in it. "Be welcome, Clear Ones, in this time and space of myself, offered freely for the Naming and Memory we share." The beginning of the old formula, the part we intone in greeting before we've all appeared.

"Yes, lovely to see you too, dear," the woman says flatly, gesturing with her cup. "Thanks for having us, I'm sure. It's not inconvenient at all."

The man smirks at her, walks over to me. "It is truly wonderful to be here with you." He kisses me on my left cheek. "Don't let her attitude ruin the mood." My right. "After all, it's not every decade we get to party with the *literal coolest* entity in the universe." He steps back, and though I maintain my smile, I am glad for the distance. His voice became chilly at the last.

"Oh, you're exaggerating, you know the Figments have a very *parochial* view of these things. They barely have a sense of the plate moving beneath their toes, much less the cosmic sweep of infinite grandeur to which we are privy." The cream and gold woman takes a sip of her drink, and her eyes narrow over its rim. "Besides, it's not so impressive when you have *three* Hearts to work with." Says the woman with only one.

"All right, you two had better leave my girl alone." The tone is joking, but there's an edge of challenge to it. Two more figures are entering the clearing together, and they're both very different from the Exemplars I greeted at the last Convocation. The speaker is a wiry woman with clear, olive skin and a waving mass of thick black hair; her jeans, artfully torn here and there, are not made for hiking, nor is the light t-shirt she wears, white with thick, forthright letters stamped on it: *Defund the Police*. Her companion is a slim young man with dark skin, short-clipped hair, and a pair of well-worn glasses that might have been trendy somewhat recently. His sweater vest, dress shirt, and slacks are nice enough, but one of his sleeves ends in a slightly frayed cuff, and the pants are faded to a lighter blue than they would have been on the rack.

They stand before me, and I wrestle down my excitement for a moment, long enough to repeat the formal greeting that my first two guests waved away.

In unison, these two respond: "All the Time that is, we Remember. All that is Us, we Name."

Then the wild-haired woman steps forward and touches my face. "It is so good to see you, little sister."

Little sister. The human words ring true, even as the sight of her foregrounds so many more relationships, so much more complexity. In a very real way, I am her progenitor, at least in part, as part of my essence flows into her, makes up part of her; in that way I am both mother and father to her. But in so many other ways, we are also lovers, in the way we intertwine infinitely in the spaces deep beneath the dirt, fingers reaching out for one another through numberless subterranean nooks. It may be simplest to say: *I love her.*

We let the feeling of togetherness hang for a moment-that-is-every-moment, then step apart. I am smiling warm and true for her. Then I look over her shoulder, and my smile is no less sincere for her companion. "Look at you!" I crow. "You haven't presented as male in practically eons."

He smiles too, and it's a shy smile, but very becoming. "This Exemplar just got hired for an important lectureship at Cornell. I thought it would be instructive to see through these eyes for a few decades. Things are happening so fast Down Below. Faster than I can remember for many years."

"Tell me about it." The woman in cream and gold sounds derisive, but she's smiling as she and the first man approach the newcomers. "Or better yet, don't. I'm *exhausted* just thinking of it." Everyone kisses and hugs, and for a moment, it is all real. The postures fall away, and we are all just *people*, whatever that means, for a moment-that-is-not, and then even that much is gone, just vapor above dark waters, and we become what we *are*, unknowable to one another but infinitely intimate, unable ever to touch but ever in contact. We are vast, and we are *together*.

Almost.

We step apart, and no one mentions the lingering absence among us. Not yet. There's still time, and none of us have ever missed a Convocation. In the meantime, there are a few other arrivals to occupy us: they start as points of light, green gold blue red violet, swirling out of the fog that is the essence of time and being. They always appear when we gather. The Minors, we have sometimes called them. Each distinct, but not quite unique. They may be what we once were, we each think, as the colored blobs dart around the clearing, deforming as they move, casting a bit of their light on a rock, a branch, one of our faces. And they may be what we will still become.

Another way in which I differ from my kind: I have Minors of my own, and now that their fellows have arrived, they emerge as well. Whatever governs the stuff of us, it has decreed that these two blobs of cosmic knowing are a little bit more like the rest of us than the five colorful orbs we have attracted. Just enough sentience sparks within them to suggest some deep and foreign wisdom, but they are enough inchoate energy as to be unpredictable, given to sudden flights of senseless disorder. Thus the forms I have helped them to assume in this little incarnation: cats.

"Wish I had me one of those," my sister says, still smiling, as the white cat and the black one bound into the circle between us all, chasing those puddles and globs of light, unsure which to follow first, then pounce, slink, stalk, and dance back out into the obscurity around us.

"I don't," says the vaguely rugged man, and we all chuckle.

Then we stop, and turn as one. A final shape has entered my clearing.

He is difficult to look at, not for any quality of his physical form, but for the uncertainty of it. He is neither young nor old, neither tall nor short. There is an obvious solidity to him, but whereas the form I have taken is what my Exemplar is learning to think of comfortably and confidently as fat, his mass is not so certain—not so much a bodily trait as a cloud he carries along with him. His left leg drags, and it is smaller, out of proportion to the rest of him. So is his face, in fact, pinched and tight-lipped on the surface of a skull that looks like it was made for big, generous features. The tint of his skin ripples on just this side of perception. The only thing about him with any definition—any truth, you could say—are his clothes: the drab grey wool of a prison officer's uniform, jacket and slacks and hat, several decades out of sync with the year we're all more or less living in Down Below.

"We can get this over with," he groans, and it's not a suggestion.

He shuffles into the circle we have formed, and we all agree silently that there is no appetite to fulfill the formal greeting. I shift uncomfortably, adjust my glasses so they're not sitting so ticklishly far down toward the tip of my nose. The next part is prescribed, and as the host of this Convocation, it is my place to begin.

"Across all of Time, we are one," I say, trying to *intone*, but it comes out a little breathlessly. "Across all of Space, we are many. Though unfathomable, our depths are known. Though nameless, long is the catalog of titles we have borne. Infinite are the possibilities that lay before us. We come together anonymous, our old names worn away like stone beneath a current. At this Convocation, we may choose again." I turn to my sister, standing at my right hand. "Clear One, how will you be known?"

Across all our multifarious existence, we have grown used to the knowledge that many things can be true at once, things that exist in opposition to one another. We have grown used to the idea that we can both be nameless, and name ourselves. That we can both name ourselves, and *draw* our names from the sensations and impressions that surround us, permeate us.

My sister looks me in the eye and with a knowing smile intones, "I am Deep."

It is true that we were born from the retreat of great shields of ice, gouging the surface of the land in their millennia-long rictus.

Deep turns to her right, where the rugged man has placed himself. "Clear One," she says, "how will you be known?"

Without missing a beat, he replies: "I am First."

It is also true that we were born from the hand of the Great One, who pressed his fingers gently into that land, leaving us as his mark.

First turns and addresses the young lecturer. "Clear One, how will you be known?" The Minors have returned by now, darting around and amongst us, my cats rubbing against shins.

"I am Marsh."

And it is true that each of us has been born to mortal parents a multitude of times, to parents rich and poor, indigenous and invasive, radical and reactionary, over and over again.

Marsh addresses cream-and-gold. "Clear One, how will you be known?"

"I am Far."

As we state our names, Memory is never distant—the Memory of names we have used before, those endlessly repeated and those worn once and then discarded, those we have shared amongst ourselves and those we have guarded jealously. Names given and names claimed. Our Minors swirl into a wall of colored energy around us as the power of Memory, the power of our knowledge of our names, our Selves, grows. My cats sit on either side of me now, their noses raised to the crackling Memory, their forms shimmering about the edges as for split-nevers they waver into squirrel and heron, into child and wildman, into tiny spark and great shadow.

Far turns to her right. Despite the ecstasy of this moment in the ritual that is the essence of who we are, I perceive the look of distaste on her face as she regards the last of us to arrive. "Clear One, how will you be known?"

The power of this act is working harshly on him. Now it is not just pigmentation that ripples, but *form itself*. In the space between one strobe-effect of existence and another, his body matches the dragging leg, and he's a small boy, whimpering in terror, and in the next space, it's that pinched face that rules, making of him a crumpled old woman with a piercing gaze. Flash, and he's a strapping man in uniform. Flash, a handsome, trendy gent lit with the reflection of amber bottles. Flash, a Black woman in cuffs, staring doggedly ahead. Flash. Flash. Flash. Flash.

"Enough!" he roars, and his form settles back into the uncertainty of the Guard-but-Not. The Minors race away, their wall of energy tearing apart in a white burst. My white cat cowers; the black hisses.

We stare. The spell—you can call it that—is not quite broken yet. It's not about the color and light, not about the ecstasy. It's about the Memory, and the naming.

The last of us pants, his body heaving. Then he spits at us: "I. Am. Bridge."

Bridge? It's not exactly an antithetical concept for us—bridges abound in the lands around us, and within our Hearts—but it's not a great fit for who we are at essence.

That's when the spell breaks. We all sag, though a tension remains palpable in the air. I feel...insubstantial. It takes a moment for me to realize that the ritual is incomplete.

"You *asshole!*" Deep is at my side. Somehow we're both on our knees; somehow, some part of her is across the circle, up in Bridge's face. "She hadn't named herself yet!"

"So let the bitch pick her name," Bridge growls, rough, weary. "The circle thing is all just show. Let her name herself! I picked mine before I ever came here today."

Deep has snapped back into herself, gathered that separate part of herself back up and wrapped it around me like a blanket. The others have all taken steps back from Bridge. Marsh looks ready to fight, and Far ready to run, though she's still the nearest to our strange cousin.

"I'm fine," I say weakly, then, with more strength, "I'm fine," but no one seems to be listening.

"You shouldn't have done that," First is muttering. "You shouldn't have done *any* of that. You shouldn't have been *able* to do that!"

"Oh, leave off." Bridge sighs painfully, moves away from the circle, and lowers himself onto an indistinct shape that may have been, Down Below, a recently fallen tree. "This tires me."

Far seems to have recovered a bit of her self-possession now that Bridge has moved off. "Yes, well. This is all *highly* unorthodox, but what are we to do? We might as well get on with it. He's right, none of this *depends* on anything. It's all just tradition." She's talking a little fast, maybe trying to convince herself. Then she looks at me. "So, what is it, dear?"

The image of a name swirls in my vision, the name I would have reached for in that moment the question and the Memory came to me. It's gone. Maybe it will come back to me at the next Convocation. Maybe I will have changed too much by then.

I shake my head clear of the haze that's invaded it. "Crooked," I say. "Just Crooked, again. It's fine."

Deep smooths my red hair back from my face. "You've kept the last name you bore," she murmurs. "It will suffice, but you have been denied your right to embody your new history."

I grip her hand, squeeze fiercely, and force a smile up at her. "History hasn't been so hot lately. Maybe it's for the best."

It's a weak joke, and I can see she doesn't accept it fully, but there's nothing to do about it now. The rest have broken the circle and are taking seats on stumps and stones around the clearing. As Deep helps me to a perch, Far waggles her fingers.

"*First?*" she snorts. "Really? Egotist."

Bridge barks a laugh. "Sing it, sister," he says, managing to mock both of them at once.

Marsh hurries to carry on with business. "Let's account for our Hearts. Crooked, maybe you should go first."

I smile appreciatively. "Thanks. Uh, I'm sure there won't be many surprises here. Three for me. Still three." Though I have been feeling a familiar old throbbing, deep down along one of my arteries. What would it be like to have *four* Hearts someday? The others would disown me.

Well, not Deep. "I am so *proud* of you," she murmurs. Then she addresses the rest: "Two Hearts here."

"I've still got Two," Marsh says, though if I had to guess, he's feeling something grow inside himself, too.

"Two as well." First is proud of what makes the others average.

Far titters. "Well, you know me. *One is the loneliest number…*"

Bridge cuts her off. "One. Let's move on."

I could pity him. We all know what it feels like to make do with one Heart, no matter how long it's been for most of us. Far makes it work by being a little bit acidic and a little bit daft and a little bit, well, far. But to be as big and full as Bridge has been for so many centuries, so many Convocations, and to hold it all within one Heart—to have no release valve in that dam regulating *feeling* and *opinion* and *conflict*...

"Well, Crooked, your Crux here is as lovely as ever." First cuts into my reverie. His discomfort with Bridge is enough to get him to overlook whatever envy he harbors towards me. "Now, how are we all doing? Still making do in the Down Below?"

Marsh smiles grimly. "If my Exemplar has to start one more email with, 'I hope you're all doing well in the midst of this difficult time...'"

"I wish that was the worst mine had to write," Deep says, and falls quiet.

The group shifts into easier conversation then. Odd, how the hard things make for easier speech. Even Far, for all her protestation of exhaustion about it, participates with a will. To begin with, about how involved we all are this time. Often, when things happen in the wider world Down Below, it's the echoes and reactions that reach us—we remember when their Towers fell, those silvery splinters that had stood for such a tiny fraction of one of our moments, but whose fall reverberated through their wires and airways, held them riveted hard, each to their many home-spots, and then the wavering waves of those who came to us after with soot in their lungs and lightning in their brains. But this time, we are a part of it all, and only a little bit because *everyone* and *everywhere* is, but even more because our Figments have been participating in the essence of it. There has been a rooting in this, too, yes, a great staying, but salted with an unyielding restlessness—they have been less like statues, shaped to stare in agony at a great terror, and more like wild wolves behind bars, pacing, pacing. And so we have been as well. And so we have waxed and waned as they have come and gone, the usual tides of their movements stuttering and uncertain, the great law Change bursting its banks and bringing with its current the fallen limbs and other detritus, the stuff of discontent, that strike and sting and uproot in their course.

That is the general thrust of the conversation, as it lasts for many nothing-moments, as my Crux orbits, over and over again, in great sweeps of nowhere-length. There is more, of course. Connected and not (though truly, everything is). Good and bad. Deep and Bridge have both mostly kept quiet as we've spoken. Bridge has only grunted in assent when one of us asks after general things, wondering if they've affected us all. Deep has offered a few lengthier anecdotes, but not much. She's holding back. I'm worried. Our growth and change have often shadowed one another's, and while I am certainly not in the best mood I've experienced in a millennia, I find myself outside my sister's anguish. I want to get on the inside, help her, shoulder some of the hurt. Finally, she lets it out.

"We talk and talk and talk. So much of it about our Figments. It didn't use to be like this. Before, we spoke more about the migrations and the hibernations. The rainfall and the aquifers. Which of us held the tallest tree. When we spoke of the Figments, it was about the minute variations in their populations. The spread in use of a new kind of bow. Casual worry that they'd taken too many deer in one season." Her eyes are closed, her fist bunched up against her thigh. "The Figments are the center of everything now. The rain falls, or doesn't fall, because of choices they made generations past. The birds come, or they don't. The deer cling on in our valleys, or emerge to be torn apart on the roads. Fine. That's fine. That's change, and change is the law. So we speak about the Figments, and their choices. The choices some of them make to hurt some others. The choices they make to hurt themselves. We rattle it off like inventories. We laugh it off like remembering an episode of *Friends*."

I feel guilty as she rages quietly. Within me, I feel my Figments hurting themselves, hurting each other. They do it in each of my thrumming Hearts.

Deep opens her eyes, breathes raggedly, takes a moment-that-is-always to look each of us in the face. Even Bridge. Especially Bridge. "We're all divided. Not us from one another—each of us, *within ourselves*. Why doesn't it *hurt* the rest of you like it does me?"

There isn't even space for a moment of shocked silence before Bridge is chuckling—an ugly sound, grimy bilge lapping at a polluted shore. "Of *course* it hurts," he wheezes.

"Well, yes," Far stumbles in on the tail of his unexpected words. "We'd be lying if we claimed we didn't feel it. What's your point?" She's wide-eyed, nearly manic, one hand flapping. "We've always hurt, haven't we? Sure, it's a little sharper now. We've felt it before. And okay, you're right, more of it is coming from within than without. That's not exactly new, either, but yes, okay, I hear you. So what do you want us to do about it?" No room to let anyone answer; she doesn't want anyone to answer. "Progress? That's the thing with you, isn't it? Ooh, *Defund the Police*. Look at that shirt. I think I liked you better as a cop! You were more boring, but at least you had sense. Progress! There's more to progress than slogans and pronouns. Do you ever stop to think about that? Ever stop to think that the pain isn't coming from any one place? There's industrial progress too, you know. Economic progress. Good jobs, good lives for our Figments. Don't those things matter to you?"

She falls silent, looking around for support, not looking at Deep. Bridge chuckles again.

Deep takes a breath, holding herself together. "I'm going to try to get past the fact that you just both-sided me there. I'm gonna go ahead and tell you that you're right. We wouldn't be hurting this bad if enterprise and industry hadn't taken a hit *all over us*. I'm not blind to that. But even *you* have to be aware of how lopsided things have gotten. And losing your job is *no* excuse to become a right-fucking-wing, autocratic, *fascist*—"

First butts in: "Oh, come on—"

"—race-baiting immigrant-hating queer-bashing *bully*. And I don't know about you, but that's at the root of the huge cracks I'm feeling -"

"Come on, you know that's an overstatement, you're exaggerating—"

Far is wearing a brittle smile now. "No, no, First, it's all right. Let her get it all off her chest. Let her tell me what she *really* thinks about me and my Figments, after all this—"

"Hey, she's not making this about you," Marsh says, at the same time that I'm saying, "You just agreed that we're *all* feeling it, this isn't—"

Far throws a hand up, disgusted. Marsh and I peter out in the face of her refusal, and Deep glares. First mutters. There's our beat, now, our calm before the storm. Then Bridge lurches to his feet.

"What, you're all going to go quiet now? This is the most interesting any of you have been in generations." The dark cloud is close upon him now. "We're just getting to the good parts. Yes, let's talk *hurt*, and *progress*. Let's talk about the great law, *change*."

He rounds on Deep. "You are such a proud little *progressive* now, aren't you? With the chanting and the milling around in the streets. Holding back the tide of wicked *authority* with your Figments's demonstrations. Hopping up and down in their little lines of electrons."

Deep brings herself up, and with her rises the penumbra of hundreds of others, the silhouette of them spiked with protest signs. "Say what you mean," she growls. And with the penumbra of her Figments, a vaster shadow rises. This isn't the ill-defined fug that clings to Bridge: she's in control. This is *her*, hanging in the air above and around and within us all—a great, ancient rent in the earth, its walls brittle and blade-like, its floor unyieldingly hard as a narrow, icy race flows through it.

Bridge crooks a smile. "Hypocrite." His hand flashes out, sharp as accusation, and Deep stumbles back, the grand display of her strength winking out. She presses her own hands to her right side, looks down, shudders. Then, from between her fingertips, a great flow of water bursts forth.

I rush forward, settle her against me as we both creak to the ground. This is not the suggestion of water that suffused the image of herself that she conjured against Bridge. This is all too real—as literal as anything can be in this space. It's real water, and it's *hot*. Hotter than the blood that sometimes issues from our Exemplars' veins.

"Is that the pain you're feeling, *sister*?" Bridge spits. "Is that a familiar ache? Progress, yes. *Progress* and its dissidents. One clique tries to take a step. Another throws down a tripwire. And still others turn away. The fever spreads. All that noise, and nothing changes. Nothing stops. You like *that* progress, Far?"

Far is shrinking away from the gouts of steaming water, soundlessly howling.

My hands are pressed over Deep's. *It burns!* I put my lips to her temple, taste the salt sweat. And I release a little bit of myself. A trickle of my cool substance. She looks up at me, grateful, frantic.

I surprise myself by speaking. "A bridge to what?"

He doesn't hear me. Marsh is pulling Far away from the aura of ill-intent washing off Bridge like loose earth in a rainstorm. "Afraid to take your dose?" he's crying after them.

"The hell is wrong with you?" First is shouting from the sidelines.

I smooth back Deep's hair, and she relaxes, nods. Pulls my hands from the gash in her side. I settle her to the ground and stand, face the edge of our tattered circle.

He's limping heavily towards Far and Marsh. "Silver-spoon snowbird bitch," he growls. "You're no better. *None of you are any better!* What do you know about hurting?"

"A bridge. To *what*?"

The others go silent. Bridge throws one lopsided shoulder back and faces me with an oily, flammable smile.

"A bridge," he says, "between enemy armies. A vast pontoon thrown across our depths. Not to unite, no." That ugly, ice-melting laugh. "Just so they can get at each other. Tear each others' throats out. To finally be done with them."

And as he turns again to dismiss me, his unremarkable little sister, I erupt.

I erupt in water and wind. I erupt in flotsam and jetsam, in words and wonder. My Minors flank me, backs arched, claws out. And I rise. I rise in a gout, an aura of pure, clean, cool liquid. From the soles of my feet, it pushes me off the ground, and I hover six feet in the air, the center of my own enclosed current. Power sloughs off my fingertips, arcs upward to my shoulders, forms a great life-giving crown around my brow.

Bridge cowers.

"It is not our place to choose the destruction of any part of us, Clear One." The voice isn't fully my own, yet I feel more myself than I have in centuries. "The law is Change, but it is not ours to make. It acts on us, as it acts on all beings and all instants." There's a flicker of feeling in my limbs, sharp but satisfying, like reaching a spot I haven't scratched in ages. "We rise and we recede. We destroy and we nourish. And as we do, we wear runnels into their lives with our presence. We leave channels in their lives by our absence." I don't have to say who *they* are; *they* are all those whose lives form like sedimentary rock in the shelter of ourselves. Now the current of water that surrounds me and crowns me is darkening, filling with more solid stuff. "*We do not choose!* Where we guide them, we do so only by the grinding of chance. Our role is as it always has been: we persist. And we *Remember.*"

The water bursts out from me like a beam of light. An angry rush, fringed with froth, and carrying with it sharp lengths of fallen timber, stones and pebbles lifted from their slumbers, gouts of earth once dry, turned now in a breath to thick, choking mud. Every square pound slams into Bridge where he stands.

He falls to his knees, and we're connected now, more than ever before, this brother of mine, this mother of mine, this son daughter enemy friend *self*. We Remember together those tiny creatures we share, those mighty beings who hurt us so. We Remember what Bridge would bring together to destroy.

Thousands of forms appear and move through us—no, millions, more. The noteworthy and the obscure. The humble and the grandiose. Our pride and our shame. A small figure bursts from me, one who claimed neither female nor male identity, but just the title *Friend*, and whose legacy still shapes the way our Figments work and wonder. From Bridge appears a dandy of a man, pompous yet kind, and from him stretches forth far distant mountains and icy winds foreign to our shores, whose joining in the great groaning union Beyond us has brought riches beyond gold. From me, a doctor holding a glass of shining violet liquid. From him, a man in a suit, his mouth opening, and from it the harmony of a thousand stirring scores. Me: a group bristling with age and wisdom and courage, faced up against a vast machine wired into the air itself (behind me, I feel the wound in Deep's side slow to a trickle). Him: a group in prison uniforms, their skin Black and Brown, faced up against a vast stone wall, their voices lifted up in righteous anger (before me, a wound opens in Bridge, but it's a necessary wound, the bone-deep sacrifice toward knowledge).

And I waver, because there is harm in us all, and for a moment-that-is-always I am a beast in a white robe and peaked hood, and superimposed over me is the slogan from a handbill, still preserved for inspection: *All roads lead to Penn Yan!* I shudder, and the nimbus of power around me and between us nearly dissolves.

But Bridge changes, too, in that moment, into a stooped Black woman, so frail and sorrowful, yet immensely powerful. She is all the more powerful to us, to *me*, because she is not of us, but *chose* us. That is within *their* power, these Figments of ours, to Choose. That is their law. Under her gaze, the Figment that I have become shrinks and billows away—not into nothingness, because the power of choice gives these strange beings, these mitochondria of ours, the capacity to make the *wrong* choice. From that capacity flows their conflict, and thus our pain.

But we Remember when they don't. And in our Beauty, we may guide them back to their Truths.

The little woman Bridge has become nods, and she fades too.

The current of water that flowed from me, with its artillery of wood and stone, splashes to the ground and is gone as if it had never been. Bridge is on his side in the earth. We are just ourselves again. But I am not Crooked anymore. I have Remembered my Name.

"Cailleach," I breathe. This name is not *of us*, either. It comes from a place and time that are nowhere near us here, now. But in it I feel the rumble of soothing storms just over the horizon. And as we know, *here* and *now* are not so very insistent.

Deep is beside me, taking my hand, pressing it. Her pain isn't gone, but I'm inside it with her now. We all are. It's bearable. As one, all of us—Deep, Marsh, First, Far, Cailleach—surround Bridge and crouch around him.

She is not who we expected him to be. Bridge is now a woman, white haired, dark eyed. I think I saw a flash of her in him before. There is a spicy warmth in the air around her for a moment, and the laughter of children, full of lessons to be re-learned. Her face is a map to many places.

"It will be my honor to greet you all at my Crux at the next Convocation," she says weakly. "I expect I won't be wearing this form then. I hope whoever I am by that time, I will know better."

"You will, Bridge," Deep says, cupping the old woman's cheek. "You already do."

Bridge smiles and fades slowly into the mist of the nowhere that surrounds us. As she does, I hear a faint counterpoint, beat within beat, and then it's gone.

They each take their leave shortly after. Deep is last. We relish a silence, entwine our fingers. Somewhere Down Below, a current overspills its banks and rushes to mingle with earth, soil, roots, leaves. Together we touch the sun. Then she's gone, too.

I look around my Crux as it seems to come into focus around me. The misty edges of things slowly close in on themselves, turning crisper and finer. My Minors tumble together through a puddle of warm light and are gone; my Exemplar will find them waiting in her modest, cozy apartment on Benham Street, just cats again (and isn't that wondrous in itself?). As the sky over the tip of the Bluff turns from indistinct grey to the most heart-wrenching, clear blue, I feel the slow, insistent thrumming of four Hearts within my chest, and savor the Memory of myself for one more moment-that-isn't: Cailleach, Crooked, two-branched Keuka, neither deep nor far but just enough for myself and everything that I am.

Villanelle
Keuka
poetry from Christine Pyanoe

She speaks to me in many ways
Her waters sparkling blue
Near her I long to spend my days

The morning comes and through the haze
Aurora lifts the dew
She speaks to me in many ways

Reflected in the sun's bright rays
The everchanging view
Near her I long to spend my days

When sadness comes, that cruel phase
I look to her anew
She speaks to me in many ways

My heart is glad beneath her gaze
My worries far and few
Near her I long to spend my days

While traveling on emerald bays
Her memory comes through
She speaks to me in many ways

Home
poetry from Sarah Pinneo Talley

Inspired by the poem 'Where I'm From' by George Ella Lyon

Where I'm from
We leave the doors unlocked
whether we're gone for a day
or a week.
Our kitchen smells like hope and fresh dough
with notes of grape jelly
and Old Spice.

Stained hands, thick and calloused
Fix the tractor, trim the grapes, pull brush
and then
drive us over hell's half acre,
clap at our recitals
and gently tuck us in at night.

'Go outside' is an executive order, rain or shine.
In the woods across the road
is a clearing under a canopy of trees.
The ground is a soft blanket of grass and pine needles,
a secret place
to share secrets with a best friend
and escape siblings
and chores.

Tiny tar bubbles form the new gravel road
because they don't pave so far out of town.
Life lessons are learned the hard way
on the bus and after class.
Sticks and stones
are for more than building forts.
One day
You might find a snakeskin

that turns out to be a snake.

Sledding is like a luge without rules or helmets.
Hold tight,
beware the gulleys
and most of all
steer clear of the deer bones on the
shortcut path to Betsy's house.
Our parents miss us only
if it's dark
and quiet.

Where I'm from
It might snow until March.
Or May.
The ground stays hard until it rains
and the mud traps your feet in place.
The snow plow comes like clockwork,
even on our dead-end country road.
The hum and rumble
in the dark early morning
is comforting somehow,
and I know
I'm home.

My Memories of Elmira, NY 1941-1946
memoir from Bard Prentiss

We are clearly shaped and refined by our experiences. We develop lifelong habits, interests, and passions that define us. Below are some of these experiences, some generic and some unique, from the first half-decade of my life.

I was born at six p.m. on Christmas Day in 1938 in St. Joseph's Hospital at Elmira, New York. My earliest date-able memory is December 7, 1941. Our paperboy told my mother and me about his brother enlisting in the Army. I think my mother cried. The level of intensity that day has planted it forever in my memory.

Shortly after that, my father, a Quaker and a conscientious objector, attempted to enlist in the Medical Corps. He was rejected because he couldn't see through a pinhole.

My mother had a victory garden in the backyard of the two-family home on Grey Street where we lived. Victory gardens were just one of countless ways to contribute to the war effort. She also had what I remember being called a victory bicycle. It had skinny tires. I believe victory bicycles were considered patriotic, since riding one saved gasoline. My father had a heavy old bike painted green that he often rode to work. They also rode on weekends for fun and during the week on errands.

During the Elmira years, we spent summers on an old farm in North Chemung, New York, that Alice Hammond, a member of our church, loaned us. It had no electricity or running water. I took baths in a washtub at the outdoor pump. My mother cooked on a wood range.

The lights were kerosene chimney lamps and a very bright Rayo lamp. My father had a large vegetable garden and trapped woodchucks in a wooden box trap that he made of scrap lumber.

One early morning when I was about three, a phoebe flew into my bedroom. I yelled, "A hebee, a hebee!" and my parents quickly came to my rescue, shooing it out the window.

The house was on a high hill, aptly called Hammond Hill, I can still remember the sound of our "pea green boat," our model A Ford sedan, as it labored up the drive in low gear. The car was named after the owl and the pussycat's "beautiful pea green boat" in a nineteenth century poem by Edward Lear.

My father was the Chemung County librarian. He was an inveterate innovator. One of his innovations while in that job was to place small lending libraries in rural corner stores around the county. He moved the books from one location to another in his car. These mini libraries were to become critical to his career, leading eventually to his becoming New York State librarian.

These corner store libraries provided a secondary, less obvious service to rural county residents. Gasoline was rationed during the war, and a trip to Elmira would have cut deeply into their monthly ration. It also benefited my father, since it qualified him for an X or unlimited rationing sticker. The generous ration it permitted allowed us to visit our summer camp on Piseco Lake in the Adirondacks.

My father was also a plane spotter. He had a set of cards that had illustrations of enemy planes from below and to the side. He would go to a designated hilltop site and scan the sky for enemy planes until relieved by another spotter.

When I was around four, my father and I walked down a path to the Chemung River. We netted ten or so inch-long bass and put them in a five-gallon aquarium containing river water on the top of a bookcase in the living room. My job was to feed them. They stayed there for quite a long time.

My parents belonged to the Chemung Valley Bird Club, and almost as soon as I could walk, I went on their birding trips. One early spring walk is vividly in my memory to this day. I was about five. The walk was on a railroad track, and on the way back someone spotted several small cylinders of dead leaves hanging from a small cherry tree. They were promethea moth cocoons.

My father always carried a case pocket knife my mother had given him, and he cut off several branch tips hosting the cocoons and brought them home. They were placed in the five-gallon tank to await hatching (the fish had either died or been released back to the river). One morning in early summer, at least one cocoon hatched, a beautiful red-brown female. That evening she flew to the screen door and soon attracted a number of gold-edged dark brown males of her species. Someone opened the screen door, and several males flew in. Our female was soon bred, and the males given their freedom. There were cherry trees at the edge of our yard, and my father was able to keep the female content until the eggs were laid.

I attribute my lifelong passion for natural history to my parents and to these early experiences.

Our next-door neighbor was Harvey Hutchinson. I think he was a school principal, but I know he was an air raid warden. His role was to walk around the neighborhood after the air raid siren blew, checking that everyone had pulled down their black shades so the city was not visible from the air. He carried a small flashlight and wore a pith helmet and tan trench coat.

During the war, metal toys were scarce and expensive. Most were made from wood. I had a wooden scooter, but an older boy down the street had a red metal one. I didn't know his name, but I envied him his scooter. More than thirty years later, I met an interesting new person in Dryden. His name was John Arneson, and as we talked it emerged that he had lived on Grey Street in Elmira and gone to Hoffman school.

When he told me where on Grey Street he had lived, I asked him if he was the owner of that red scooter. He said he was. He was only a year older than I, but at five, that's twenty percent.

My kindergarten teacher was Miss Straley. She was a wonderful introduction to my education. She must have loved kids, and every day was a joy. She had a boyfriend in the Air Corps and he provided a cardboard mockup of the instrument panel of a bomber. They got large cartons and arranged them to look like the fuselage of an airplane. In that plane-like construction they put our desks, and from then on we had our desk time in the plane.

As an expression of youth support for the war effort and to start us young in the habit of saving, school children were encouraged to buy defense stamps. We took money to school once a week and bought the stamps, which we pasted in a book. I believe each full book equaled a $25.00 savings bond.

Evenings at home were centered around an old Philco radio. Before supper, I got to listen to *Tom Mix*, *Tennessee Jed*, and, I think, *The Lone Ranger*. After supper, listening became a family thing. The news with Lowell Thomas supported by W. W. Chaplin in London and a host of less memorable reporters.

During the war, scrap drives were common. Cans were crushed, collected and melted down to become the machines of war. Scrap paper and old newspapers were-recycled into I know not what, for the war effort. Milkweed down was also collected, perhaps for insulation. Schoolchildren were enlisted to collect recyclables of all sorts, and I opted to collect old newspapers. I would walk around the neighborhood pulling my wooden wagon and collecting newspapers. There was no TV, and the newspaper was the principal purveyor of "in-depth" news, so most everyone "took the paper." It's probably a gross exaggeration, but as I remember it I nearly filled our garage.

One of my favorite toys was what we called a screw bomb. We would cut off the blue tips of kitchen matches and place a few of them in a nut that had been screwed a couple of threads onto one of two bolts. We started the other bolt in the open end of the nut, snugly but not tightly. We would throw this unit at the sidewalk. The impact usually exploded the match heads, providing a pleasingly loud noise.

On VJ Day my mother gave me money to go to the store on Hoffman Street and buy a big box of kitchen matches and the necessary hardware to build a couple of screw bombs. Screw bomb play entertained me for the afternoon, and that evening my father took me downtown to watch the celebrations. My mother stayed home with my little brother. People threw confetti and rolls of toilet paper from second story windows. It was very exciting. My father, in the heat of the moment and totally out of character, exclaimed: "All the whores are out tonight." I asked what whores were and his answer, if he answered at all, is lost to my memory.

In 1946, my father received a job offer from the State Library in Albany to head their Traveling Libraries Division. The fall before we moved to Albany, my parents sold the pea green boat and bought a 1939 Chevy coupe from our next-door neighbors, the Bakers.

I was on the verge of adding a new and exciting collection of life experiences. Life was good in East Schodack and Brokview, New York, but that's another decade and another story.

Christmas Miracle: Nativity Scene in Virgil, NY
poetry from Carolyn Clark

The boys' and girls' entrances on the closed school,
goats and sheep perched on snowbanks
in the side yard of an old white house by the fire department sign
a Shetland pony stands at the door
at 6 degrees Fahrenheit
the wind drifting the snow from the public graveyard
onto a road that winds before time
like a magic carpet leading to the nearby resort
a mist is thick with snowmaking,
trees glistening gray and golden
as a Bruegel landscape.

October Storm
poetry from Ron Bailey

a freeze last night
snaps strength of stem grip
leaves torrent toward earth

i sit with coffee in a folding chair
in the garden
near norwegian maples
next to hostas ready for the blade

leaves land on my thighs
on my arms
veins on my skin
between neck and collar . . .
no pulse

orange and yellow seep
my bones
turn blood to syrup
ribs will glow in the dark

i am drenched
to my breath
in autumn

Gift on East Lake Rd.
poetry from Joan Mistretta

Long corridor of flowers,
   now forsythia,
   later day lilies.
Planted on purpose
   along a busy country road
   connecting two towns.

They must have conspired,
   the nice folks with their lake houses,
   to plant up by the road for us,
   their neighbors
On our way from here to there,
   passing the lucky ducks.

Two Hundred Years and Counting
poetry from Daphne Solá

Two hundred years ago,
a time of barn dances, hay-wagons
and horse-drawn ploughs,
it was just a waltz up the road
to the house the Van Cuyks built
midway down a sloping hill
that ends in a spring-fed stream
that, in turn, feeds the pond
where the blue heron comes each summer
flying in long slow circles
until he lands at the edge of the pond
and proceeds to walk like a dancer
all along the banks,
sliding each foot into the water
slow-motion, causing no ripples,
until he sees and snares an unsuspecting fish
snatched horizontally in his beak
and soon jostled around
and swallowed . . .
just another evening's tasty dinner
We watch, then turn
towards the setting sun
and climb the hill
for our own dinner
in the Van Cuyks' house
which, for a time
we will call our own.

The Memory of Water
lyric essay from Laura Dennis

Green

"Close your eyes," the instructor said. "Now think about your green. This will be your green."

Mine appeared so quickly that I wondered if had been waiting for me all along.

"Now take your plate and go get your paint."

I picked up the blue plastic plate that was to serve as a palette. *Water and sunlight make a lake*, I thought. As if reading my mind, the teacher said, "Blue and yellow make green." Then she added "…but what else might you need?"

I had no idea, so I followed my classmates' lead and pumped dollops of black and white onto the empty spaces on my plate.

I know little about how art is made other than random facts learned in museums, books, and school. I do, however, remember the color wheel. And I keep the memory of water with me wherever I go.

Generally speaking, words are both my preferred medium and my muse. My friend Alisa, however, had talked me into taking this painting class, assuring me that neither experience nor ability were required. Still, my fingers shook slightly as they tried to find purchase on these unfamiliar tools. I breathed into the moment, letting the palette knife, like a pen, become an extension of my hand. I watched the colors swirl together, adding ever smaller dabs until, at last, my hand stilled in wonder. There it was, recollection made reality, almost as if I were sitting out on a dock, not in an art studio miles and worlds away.

Background

Imitating the instructor's deft wrist movements as best I could, I began applying my green to the canvas in broad, swooping strokes. Nostalgia unfurled as the canvas filled. Class picnics at Indian Pines. The splash of sodden sneakers during cross country practice at Red Jacket Park. Motor boats and inner tubes. Stolen kisses and broken hearts. The painting's texture changed as memories flooded in. In the upper right-hand corner, where the teacher had used a smudge of black, I had, almost unconsciously, chosen a deep gemstone blue.

I floated in a comforting, deliquescent peace as I sipped a cup of coffee and looked at what I'd already done. The green expanse seemed to flow from that corner whose hue matched those elongated, glacier-cut sapphires known as the Finger Lakes. I thought back to the time I'd described them that way to a friend. Thoughtfully, she'd replied, "You know, I can see that… but for some reason, I've always thought of lakes as green."

On my next trip north, I'd put this observation to the test. My friend and I were both right–the lake was indeed green…and blue…and also brown and yellow and gray. Captivated, I'd written a piece in which I'd tried to capture every shade and tone the lake had revealed. My first readers deemed this overkill, and rightly so. My lexical abundance had buried the lake that I so wanted to bring to life. How to capture the million things that happen when light meets water, the way those iridescent moments shimmer in the soul? I decided I would try again the following summer…which, it turned out, would be 2020. How long can colors last before the ebb and flow of memory wash them away?

Purple

"Now think about your sphere," the instructor said. "What color do you want it to be? It can be anything."

This time, I chose purple. I had nothing particular in mind—I just really love the color purple.

I soon found myself, however, wishing I'd been more precise, imagined, for example, fields of lavender or the stain of a freshly crushed grape. I fumbled with the palette knife, stirring in one color then another, until I came up with a grayish violet that felt vaguely familiar. Many months would pass before I realized that it lines the tiny shells strewn along the beaches of Keuka Lake.

Sphere

Another artist in the class taught those interested how to free-hand a circle. Mercifully, this was not required—templates had also been provided. Knowing that I couldn't draw so much as a line without it wobbling, I dutifully taped the cutout to my canvas. I then dipped a brush in my newly created purple paint. The template should have made it easy to produce a perfectly rounded sphere.

"Should" is the operative word.

By the time I was done, my circle had escaped the confines of its white posterboard frame. A fuzziness here. A lumpiness there. The result was an almost-sphere. A sphere from a distance...as long as you didn't get too close. I swallowed the lump of frustration that threatened to close my throat. The nervous murmurs of my classmates told me I was not alone.

Later, in the car, I would glance at the painting resting on the seat next to me. As I waited for a light to turn, a thought came. *The sphere is me.* I blinked in confusion as my eyes dimmed with unbidden tears. I had no idea what those words might mean.

Shading

Before that car ride, we had two last steps to complete. First, the teacher said, we would add shading to our sphere. She demonstrated as she talked, nimbly adding a splash of black here, a streak of white there.

Although I was still trying to smooth my circle, I shifted my attention to the daubs of paint remaining on my plate. Added to my painting, they continued to look exactly like what they were–splotches of black and white. No elegantly blended patches of light and shade for me. Maybe my shade of purple was to blame–it suddenly looked terribly gray. Reminding myself that I was a learner, not a master, I kept at it, smoothing the lumps, blending the blotches and lines. When I look at the painting now, I would almost say the shading works.

Almost.

Shadow

The last step–creating our sphere's shadow–proved to be the most difficult of all. I listened. I watched the teacher, then classmates seated nearby. I positioned a brush to serve as a horizon, just as we'd been shown. I called the teacher over. Although she did not say as much, it seemed my light source was ill-defined. She made a few suggestions. I did my best to follow them. Finally, I laid my brush down in defeat. I'd not given my sphere a shadow. Instead, it sported something suspiciously like a tail.

Who wants to see their shadow anyway? I grumbled, not all that deep in my mind. *I'll stick with water and light.*

The next day, Alisa messaged me.

Alisa: Yesterday was fun

Me: Yeah it was

Alisa: You should post a picture of your painting

Me: IDK. It's not that good

Alisa: Do it. Mine photographed far better than it actually is

Me: Lol. We'll see

Then, not having anything to lose, I did it. I snapped a pic. Alisa was right. The tail looked less like an appendage and more…dare I say it… a shadow. I remembered my reaction in the car the day before, those unexpected tears I'd not let fall.

Ending where we began

The class had been billed as an experience in art therapy for those who have experienced or work with trauma. For some of my classmates, the release had been immediate, the emotions flowing from body to brush to canvas, looping over and back again. One woman all but broke down and wept right there in the middle of class. For me, however, it was at that stoplight that a conversation of sorts began, one that has continued ever since.

The original assignment had been to create a stationary sphere in a field of green, lit as if from beyond the canvas, its shadow revealing its exact position in the larger world. My sphere, however, seems to be on the move. It makes me wonder if the black part is a tail after all, a way of propelling the sphere through its aqueous space. At the same time, I do see a shadow, that of something…someone… streaming up from the depths, stretching toward the light. The sphere's lumps and dents now strike me less as imperfections and more as evidence that it does not know who or what it wants to become. Perhaps it wants simply to dissolve into water and light, end as it began, adrift in a wash of color. Maybe that is what it means to come home.

Looking at an Old Photograph of a Seneca Falls Baseball Team
poetry from Dewey Hill

Dad's catcher's mitt catches my attention
Puffed up like a pillow,
and plopped down
in front of the squatting catcher:
It is 1920; Dad is 22.

Dad lived in a tent on a Cayuga Lake shoreline,
A tent pitched too close to rising water,
And while he slumbered,
slowly seeped in water
that soaked him
and
dampened his day.

And just so has seeped the cold
into the lives
of every teammate
in this photo
And of every lively, cheering fan
who once watched Dad raise that pillowed mitt
to tag the runner
OUT
at home plate.

These elderly days,
I sense the cold Cayuga
silently seeping into my own tent.

And in my dreams:
I'm heading home,

Hoping to beat the tag.
Hoping to bat just a few more times
before the end of the game.

Dewey Hill, my father, went on after his time playing for Seneca Falls to a life in baseball, catching for Toronto, Buffalo, Atlanta, Montreal in the International League, and then for the House of David that played in every state of the union and every province in Canada. The old photograph that inspired this poem can be found at the Seneca Falls Historical Site on Facebook.

Road Remedy
poetry from Agnes McClear

If going through hell, keep going, I have read
But where exactly does a person go?
The hardest part is getting out of bed.

Brush teeth, comb hair, get dressed, and come, you said
We'll wander where the Riesling grapevines grow
If going through hell, keep going, I have read.

I face Thanksgiving with a sense of dread
(His empty captain's chair's the worst, you know)
The hardest part is getting out of bed.

Don't cook, you say, let Belhurst cook instead!
A castle-prepared feast, lake view below
If going through hell, keep going, Churchill said.

Soon winter's shadows seep into my head
I try to smile, not let my sorrow show
The hardest part is getting out of bed.

Let's drive to Naples for a pie! you said.
The rolling hills are shining with fresh snow
If going through hell, keep going, I have read

If I want pie, I'll *have* to leave my bed.

Old Friend
poetry from Gary Snook

I found your antlers
Deep in the woods
So I know you made it
Through another year
No bullet or arrow
Has ever found you
It seems only time
That ceaseless hunter
Will ever track you down
It's been some time
Since I saw you last
Watching across the field
Your tail flicking danger
And yet you feel
Like an old friend
One I hope to see soon
Under slated skies
Loosing flakes so heavy
You can hear them
Strike the trees
Or better still
Watching cautiously
As is your custom
Across a greening field
Through the opening buds
Of a newborn April day

Manure Pile Muse
poetry from Carolyn Clark

Two false cognates
—*burgeon* and *bourgeois*—
spring to mind
as each fewer manure pile
multiplies with flies.
I shovel gingerly,
grateful my back is now
bending in ways
that didn't work last spring.

We've come all the way,
from manic May
to quirky October.
The first frost is late,
yet leaves are somehow bright,
no thanks to climate change
in this our region - Finger Lakes (FLX).
More people are moving here,
Some coming back
from Los Angeles (LAX)
to our lush, green Arcadia—Newfield, NY.

Like manure-pile flies,
we burgeon as the new bourgeoisie,
cell phones in hand, even me—
musing through the morning chores
making less room for more,

just one stop away from extinction.

bur·geon /ˈbərjən/

verb

gerund or present participle: **burgeoning**

begin to grow or increase rapidly; flourish.

"manufacturers are keen to cash in on the burgeoning demand"

o ARCHAIC•LITERARY

put forth young shoots; bud.

Origin:: Middle English: from Old French *bourgeonner* 'put out buds', from *borjon* 'bud', based on late Latin *burra* 'wool'.

bour·geois /ˈboorZHwä/

adjective

adjective: **bourgeois**

1. of or characteristic of the middle class, typically with reference to its perceived materialistic values or conventional attitudes.

"a rich, bored, bourgeois family"

mid-16th century: from French, from late Latin *burgus* 'castle' (in medieval Latin 'fortified town'), ultimately of Germanic origin and related to *borough*. Cf. *burgess*.

The Way of the Lake
poetry from Carol Mikoda

I walk the quiet road that lines the lake,
always wondering. Swallows slip above
the water, sewing their paths from dock to dock,
as I stop to sit awhile and ask the lake,
"Why am I here?" Purple martins chirp
and trill, pink phlox tremble, tulips
nod their spent heads, but the lake does not
respond. I ask, "Why me?" No answer
but breezes squeezing between leaves, and shrieks
of gulls. I ask, "Why now?" Confirmed
by dawn's warmth, by noontime blaze, and again
by sunset's blood lapping gently at the dusk,
the lake finally speaks: "There is only now."

The Great Roseland Indignity
fiction from John Buchholz

Hello. My name is Corky McPherson, and everybody in town knows what happened at our ninth-grade picnic last June, so I might as well tell you, and I might as well start at the beginning.

Excitement spread like a forest fire when Mr. Atkins announced that the picnic would be held at Roseland, that big amusement park over on Canandaigua Lake. My imagination immediately conjured up the merry-go-round and its shiny horses with their long, flowing manes and red nostrils, prancing to the brassy music of the big Wurlitzer band organ. And I could hear the claps of the shooting-gallery rifles and the clangs of the steel bullets hitting their targets. And I could see the bumper cars in their pavilion, whirling and colliding like drunken ladybugs, golden sparks spewing from the metal ceiling over their heads.

And everywhere—on the miniature golf course, in the penny arcade, on the Whip, and on the long space rockets that circled gracefully out over the lake—I saw Lauren Sutherland, the new girl in our class. And I pictured me holding her hand.

She had soft blue eyes, delicate lashes, and pale freckles that sprinkled her cheeks. Her flaxen hair swept her shoulders, and her delicate curves and Ipana-white smile melted me.

Somehow, before somebody else got to her, I had to work up the courage to ask her to go to the picnic with me. But I was sure she'd turn me down. She was pedigreed, and her parents had just bought the big Healy place up on the hill outside of town. She was fluent in French, had a horse, talked about Broadway shows, and wrote book reports about sophisticated stuff like the rise and fall of the Roman Empire. And I don't think she'd ever noticed me.

I'd never asked a girl for a date before, and I spent all morning agonizing about what I should say.

Hi, Lauren. My name is Corky. Your hair looks very nice. I was just wondering if you'd like to go to the picnic with me.

Or, *Pardon me, Lauren. We've never met. I'm Corky. How's your horse? Would you go to the picnic with me?*

Or, *Hi, Lauren. My name is Corky, and some of my friends thought I should ask you to go to the picnic with me. So what do you think?* Nothing seemed right.

Whenever she glanced my way during class, I smiled and hoped her eyes would meet mine, but they always swept right past me and back to her books. I thought about slipping a note into her locker out in the hallway. *Dear Lauren, You don't know me, but I'm in your class. My name is Corky, and if you'd meet me at the drinking fountain outside the gym after school today, I'd like to talk with you about something. I'm quite tall and I'll be wearing a blue shirt.*

But then I decided that a note wasn't a good idea. She might show it to her friends or my friend Jimmy.

&

Lauren was right behind me as a bunch of us exited algebra class just before lunch, and I was tempted to say something, but it wasn't the right time. I needed privacy, I just wasn't ready, and she was laughing and talking with Helen Drummond.

Halfway through lunch, I spotted her sitting with some girls over on the other side of the cafeteria, and Jimmy poked me. "How come you're staring at Lauren Sutherland?"

"I'm not staring at her," I said.

"Well, I been talkin' to you for two minutes and you never heard a word I said."

"Well, I'm not starin' at her."

"She's goin' to the picnic with Butch Collins, you know."

"What? You kiddin' me?"

"Nope. That's what I heard."

"But did he ask her yet?"

"How do I know? You think I'm a mind-reader? How come you always ask me stupid questions?"

I knew I had to act fast, so after school I waited for Lauren near the lockers. Two or three minutes went by, and then I saw her walking toward me through the crowd with some other girls. It was now or never. I spit on my hand and slicked down my cowlick, and as Lauren walked by, I opened my mouth, but nothing came out. Then, when she was twenty feet beyond me, I managed to shout her name, but it cameout like a yodel, and as it echoed down the hallway, the girls stopped and stared back at me.

I cleared my throat. "Lauren," I blurted out, "could I please talk with you for a minute?"

She pointed at herself with a puzzled look. "Me?"

I nodded. "Just for a minute?"

Annette Goodman rolled her eyes and Tootsie Garafolo snapped her gum as Lauren walked toward me. She smiled that perfect white smile, and my hands trembled and I swallowed. "Hi, Lauren. My name is Corky, and I was thinking that it might be nice if you and me...no, *I, us*...uh, *we*...went to the pickland at Rosenic together. No.

Pisnic at Roseland. No. Excuse me. *Picnic*. What do you think?"

Sweat trickled down from my armpits and Lauren giggled as she looked out the window, then back at me. "Well, maybe," she said, smiling. "I'll let you know tomorrow. O.K.?"

I studied her face for a sign of promise, but saw none. "Tomorrow?"

"Yes, sometime tomorrow," she said, turning and walking back toward Annette and Tootsie. "Excuse me. I have to catch the bus now."

"Maybe tomorrow morning?"

"Maybe," she said over her shoulder.

&

First thing the next morning, from down the hallway, I saw something white hanging on my locker door and scurried toward it. It was a small sealed envelope with "Corky" neatly printed on it. My pulse raced as I looked up and down the hallway, popped the envelope open, and pulled out a note.

"Dear Corky," it said. "Thank you for the invitation. I will attend the picnic with you, but will pay my own expenses. I'll meet you at the bus next Saturday. Sincerely, Lauren." Below her name was a postscript.

"My mother sends her best regards to your mother, with whom she enjoyed a pleasant conversation at last month's Civic Club meeting."

My heart thumped, and as I hurried past the boys' lavatory looking for Jimmy, I heard singing and pulled the door open. He and the Nesbitts were standing beside the stalls with heads tilted back like baby birds begging for worms. They were warbling "Sioux City Sue" in three-part harmony, and although the Nesbitts didn't have much else going for them, they sure could sing.

I couldn't contain my excitement, and I held the note up in front of Jimmy's face. Still singing, he leaned forward and squinted at it, snatched it from my hand, and read it.

"How come she's goin' to the picnic with a drip like you when she could be goin' with Collins?"

I couldn't come up with an answer that would satisfy Jimmy, so I said nothing, grabbed the note, and stuck it in my pocket.

"Hey, what's that?' Nelson Nesbitt said, picking at a pimple on his nose. "What's goin' on?"

"Sutherland's goin' to the picnic with this idiot," Jimmy said. "Do you believe it?"

"I knew I shoulda ast her," Nelson said, stomping his foot. "Damn! I shoulda ast her. She'da gone with me!"

"She wouldna gone with you, you geek," Jimmy said. "You're a bigger jerk than *he* is!"

&

The bus was scheduled to leave at 8:30 from in front of the school, and I was one of the first to arrive. I wore dungarees, loafers, and my white windbreaker over a short-sleeved plaid shirt. Bobby Nordini was there with Henry Fredericks, and Helen Knapp stood behind them, jabbering with some other girls. Down the street, Jimmy and the Numb Nesbitts hopped off their bikes and pushed them into the racks in the parking lot.

Henry peered out from under the bill of his Brooklyn Dodgers cap. "How much you bring, McPherson?"

"Three bucks," I said.

"Just three bucks? My old man gave me five!"

I waited for a few seconds and then, as limply as I could, I said, "Five bucks. Wow."

"Yessir-e-e-e!" He exclaimed. "Five smackers!" Beaming, he looked at Bobby, then back at me. "You takin' anybody today?"

I was surprised he hadn't heard. "Yeah, I sure am." I stuffed my hands into my jacket pockets and gazed up at the Methodist church steeple that towered above the maple trees across the street.

"Well," Henry said, "who?"

"You didn't hear?" I paused, then slowly curled her name off my tongue. "Law....ren....Suth....er....land."

Henry shook his head in astonishment, then stared down at his black-and-white U.S. Keds. "Lauren Sutherland?! Holy cripes! Lauren Sutherland?!"

Bobby gazed down the street as a big yellow school bus rumbled toward us. "Here it comes!" he announced. "And there's Sutherland's old man's car right behind it!"

I'd never seen Lauren's father, and had hoped that her mother would bring her. The shiny black Oldsmobile Rocket 88 purred to a stop at the curb behind the bus, and a tall, athletic-looking man in a dark suit stepped out and scanned the crowd through wire-rimmed glasses. The sun glinted off the car's windshield, and my heart hammered as I made out Lauren's face through the glass.

"Holy cripes!" Henry said as Jimmy and the Numb Nesbitts approached. "He's a big bruiser, ain't he? Don't he look just like Clark Kent?"

Jimmy walked up, nodding toward the Oldsmobile. "Hey, McPherson. That's Sutherland's old man over there."

"You think I don't know that, you idiot?" I said.

"Yeah, well, I heard he played football for Cornell, so you better mind your manners with his little girl today or he'll kick your face in."

Mr. Sutherland opened Lauren's door, and as she stepped out, she smiled up at him and a breeze fluttered a strand of her hair across her face. She wore dungarees and a white blouse and jacket, and her lips were the color of my mother's little pink tea roses.

"Oh, man, McPherson," Henry muttered. "Where'd you get all the luck?"

"Well, whadya waitin' for, stupid?" Jimmy said. "Get over there and meet her old man. See if you can make a good impression, and try not to stumble on the way." He threw a quick grin at the Nesbitts, and they all chortled in harmony.

Lauren shaded her eyes and turned toward me as I approached. "Hi, Corky. I'd like you to meet my father." She smiled up at him again, and as inconspicuously as I could, I wiped the sweat from my right palm onto my pants. "Daddy, this is my friend Corky."

"Nice to meet you, Corky," he said, shaking my hand and smiling. "Nice day for the picnic."

"Sure is," I responded. "Nice to meet you, sir."

"Well, I'd better run," he said, turning toward his car. "Have a good time, and please say hi to your dad. I met him at the Chamber of Commerce meeting a few weeks ago. Very nice man."

Lauren waved at him, and as the Oldsmobile slipped away from the curb, I turned, smiled at her, and said, "Your father looks a lot like Superman."

&

The bus ride to Roseland was like a wonderful dream, and I wanted it to go on forever. All of my worries about conversing with Lauren had been in vain. Whenever there were lapses, she asked what my hobbies were, or if I liked algebra, or if the Rochester Royals were my favorite basketball team. And sometimes, as the bus swayed around a sharp curve, her shoulder would brush against me or her knee would touch mine, and a sugary warmth flooded through me.

Jimmy, Bobby, Henry and the Numb Nesbitts sat at the rear of the bus, and whenever I caught them eyeballing Lauren, I sailed a gloating grin at them and they responded by sticking out their tongues and making faces at me.

&

Canandaigua Lake sparkled through the trees along the shore as the bus pulled into the parking lot. Roseland was as colorful and exciting as I'd remembered it from the summer before. As we stepped down from the bus, a warm breeze wafted in from the lake and tousled Lauren's hair. She brushed it from her face and turned and smiled. "Hear the music?"

I nodded. A chorus of tinkling bells, tweeting piccolos, wheezing reeds, crashing brass cymbals, and thumping bass drum floated in from the distant merry-go-round.

"It's kind of warm," Lauren said. "Want to leave our jackets on the bus?"

"O.K.," I said, and returned them to our seat.

We all stood beside the bus as Mr. Atkins distributed our amusement-ride tags. "We've reserved some tables under the trees near the big speedboat dock," he announced, "and lunch will be served promptly at noon, thanks to the wonderful efforts and generosity of the Freshman Mothers. And I'm sure I don't have to remind you," he continued, "that our school will be judged by your comportment today, so please behave like the fine young ladies and gentlemen you are, have a good time, and remember to report to the picnic area at noon."

As Lauren and I walked across the parking lot with Kenneth Hanover and Norma Simmons, I could see my favorite ride off in the distance, down by the willows near the lake, and I knew that if my shooting-gallery or miniature-golf skills didn't impress her, I could win her heart as we soared together on the Flying Scooters. I had figured out how to maneuver them the previous summer, and was determined to give her a ride she'd remember for the rest of her life.

Kenneth and Norma disappeared after the four of us had ridden on the merry-go-round and Whip and bumper cars, and as Lauren and I walked to the penny arcade, I suggested that we stop at the hot dog stand. I was very hungry. I'd been so nervous about my date with her that I couldn't eat anything the night before, and had skipped breakfast, too.

"Aren't you afraid you'll spoil your appetite for the picnic?" she said. "We're going to eat in about two hours."

"I can't wait. I'm awful hungry," I said, and I ordered a porker, some french fries, and a root beer.

After I'd wolfed the food down, we joined some other kids for a speedboat ride down the east side of the lake. Phil Boice and Hilda French sat on the seat just ahead of us, and they made out pretty much the whole way. Everybody tried to ignore them, but it was impossible, and I knew that Lauren was embarrassed because she blushed and grimaced and turned toward me and dropped her eyes and whispered, "My goodness."

I'd already sneaked my right arm along the back of Lauren's seat, and had thought about lightly touching her shoulder like it was accidental, but decided not to. I was afraid she'd think I was trying to pull the same stuff as Phil, and besides, my hand was all sweaty.

Later, at the shooting gallery, I knocked down four ducks and snuffed out three candles, and got the feeling that I might have scored a few points with Lauren. But she was hard to read, so I wasn't sure.

Then we rode on the bumper cars, Whip, and merry-go-round again, and just before noon, as I finished a bag of popcorn, we sailed out over the water on the space rockets that circled the big tower standing at the edge of the lake.

&

The Freshman Mothers had prepared a big picnic, and although I was hungry when we sat down, I thought I might have eaten too much when we finished. In addition to the hot dog, potato salad, baked beans, and apple pie, I'd downed another bottle of root beer, and my stomach was feeling a bit uncomfortable.

While Lauren talked with Carol Short, I leaned aside and burped as quietly as I could. Then, as I let my belt out two notches, I heard shrieks and saw bright colors zipping behind the treetops down toward the far end of the park near the miniature golf course.

I leaned over toward Lauren and pointed at the trees. "See the Flying Scooters over there?"

"Wow!" she said. "They look pretty scary!"

"Well, come on. Let's go." I reached out and took her hand. "You're going to have a ride you'll never forget!"

I was still holding her hand as we approached the low fence surrounding the ride. Cabled to a giant rotating wheel atop a tall tower, eight shiny, bulbous orbs with large front fins swooped by overhead.

"I don't know," Lauren said, gazing upward and wincing. "Looks very scary."

"It's very safe, Lauren," I said. "It's been here for years, and it never had an accident. Looks like it was built with a big Erector set, doesn't it?"

She withdrew her hand from mine and rubbed her arm. "Very scary looking."

"Aw, don't worry. It'll be fun. Come on. You'll love it."

The ride operator stood at a control panel along the fence, and as he idled the engine, the scooters gradually drifted to a stop and dangled two feet above the pavement. Laughing, Tootsie, Annette, Bobby, Henry, and some others climbed out of their scooters and staggered toward the exit gate. As Henry swayed past, he took off his Dodgers cap, wiped his forehead and rolled his eyes at us. "Holy cripes!" he exclaimed. "That's the best ride I ever been on!"

I helped Lauren into a cherry-red scooter, climbed in next to her, and tested the big steering fin mounted on the front to be sure it maneuvered easily. Over on the tower's other side, Jimmy sat with Helen Iberius in an orange scooter that matched his hair. He threw me a big grin and a thumbs-up as the Nesbitts sat bobbing in a blue scooter right behind him. Their mouths were wide-open and moving in unison, and I knew they were singing.

When all the scooters were filled, the attendant checked safety bars and made a few adjustments, then walked to the control panel and pushed a big button. The electric motor whined, the overhead circular girder system groaned and surged forward, and all the scooters abruptly lifted and shot ahead in unison.

My stomach felt like it was four feet behind me, and I turned to my left and belched as Lauren screeched and grabbed the safety bar as the sudden acceleration pinned us against the back of our seat. I looked over the side at the tarmac below as the superstructure creaked. Within seconds, the overhead cables were straining at maximum and the scooters were sailing at top speed.

I turned toward Lauren. The color had drained from her face, her brow was furrowed, and her eyes were thin slits aimed straight ahead. Her jaw was jutting, her lips were tightly sealed, and her golden hair was flying behind her.

I bellowed "Isn't this great, Lauren?!" into her left ear, but she didn't respond, so I decided that it was time to impress her with my maneuvering skills. Cackling, I jammed the rear of the big steering fin as far toward Lauren as it would go, and the scooter dove to the left and swooped downward.

At the dive's low point, as the cables slapped taut and jarred my teeth and twisted the scooter violently from side to side, Lauren shrieked, "Stop it, Corky! Stop it!"

I roared, and for two full revolutions, we circled at tarmac level. As onlookers lining the fence below whizzed past in a blur, I beamed, waved, and shouted, "Whooo-eee!" Then, quickly yanking the fin all the way to the left, I sent us aloft again, swooping toward the trees that surrounded the ride.

"Corky!" Lauren screamed, "stop it!"

But I knew she didn't mean it, and I reared back and howled, pushed the fin all the way to the right again, and the scooter plunged into another nosedive.

Then I aimed it skyward again, and as we sailed toward the treetops, Lauren shrieked, " I mean it, Corky! Stop doing that! Get me off this thing!"

It was then, with Lauren pummeling my shoulder and screaming, that I suddenly began to feel queasy.

"O.K.! All right!" I shouted, and returned the scooter to its normal path. But my dizziness spun out of control. Treetops spiraled crazily past and boats out on the lake looped across the water.

Gripping the scooter's door with both hands, I leaned over and took a deep breath, belched ominously, and tried to focus on the big central pylon, hoping to stabilize my insane world. But as the tower undulated, my face turned cold and I felt nausea building in my stomach.

I prayed that the ride would end and I could leap over the fence, bolt for the trees, and vomit in privacy.

In utter despair, I glanced to my right as the scooter raced at top speed. "Lauren!" I shouted. One wide eye peered at me from under the wild yellow hair plastered to her face. "Lauren!" I shouted again, the wind whooshing past and my stomach bubbling with urgent distress. "I don't feel very well! I think I'm going to throw—"

It was then that a technicolor explosion of root beer, hot dog bits, popcorn, mustard, french fry fragments, potato salad chunks, baked beans, apple pie pieces, and relish spewed from my mouth into the warm afternoon air.

The horrible stew seemed suspended in front of Lauren for a moment, then hit her full in the face. As she shrieked and pawed at the mess, I lurched across her lap and disgorged another kaleidoscopic eruption over the side, and horrified onlookers below raced in all directions.

I hung there retching and hucking and spitting, and as Lauren punched and clawed and screeched awful names at me, the big motor died and the scooters drifted back to earth. Picking at her hair and still shrieking, she leaped from the scooter and raced into the arms of some Freshman Mothers, who quickly ushered her away.

I looped past the open gate, wiping my eyes and dabbing at my mouth with my shirttail, and the crowd parted like the Red Sea. A tall man standing at the rear was the only one who spoke as I passed through. "You all right, kid?"

"I don't know. Maybe," I said, and staggered to the lake, knelt, cupped my hands and splashed cool water on my face. Then I rinsed out my mouth, took off my shirt, sloshed it around, and wrung it out.

When I began to feel a bit better, I got up, spread my shirt on a big boulder and sat down under a willow. As I watched the lake lap at the shore, a flat stone skipped over the water twenty feet out, and a voice behind me said, "Hey, Cork. You feelin' any better?"

It was Jimmy, and he walked toward me, stooped, and picked up another stone. "Yeah," I said. "A little better."

"Sure feels good to puke and get it over with, don't it?"

"Yeah, but have you seen Lauren any place?"

"She's gone. One of the mothers took her home."

"I sure messed that one up, didn't I?"

"Don't worry about it. Another minute on that ride and she'da puked her lunch all over you!"

&

As the bus pulled away from the park, Mr. Atkins walked back and patted my shoulder. "That certainly was an unfortunate incident, Charles, but I'm happy you're feeling better."

A few minutes later, somebody up toward the front hollered, "Corky McBarf! Corky McBarf!" and all the kids laughed. Mr. Atkins stood immediately and said, "I don't want to hear any more of that! Do you understand?" and all was quiet during the rest of the trip home.

&

Lauren was absent from school on Monday, and I slid a note into her locker through the vent slots. "Dear Lauren, I'm very very sorry for what happened last Saturday, and I hope you will forgive me. I had a very good time until I got sick, and I thank you for going to the picnic with me. Sincerely, Corky."

But Lauren didn't respond, and on Tuesday, during algebra class, I saw her exchanging smiles and notes with Butch Collins. And whenever I passed her and Tootsie and Annette in the hall, they looked the other way and scurried off in silence.

&

On the last day of school, after we had picked up our report cards, Jimmy and the Nesbitts and I walked down to Hank's Soda Shoppe to celebrate. We all ordered Mexican sundaes, and as Hank's wife brought them over, the front door opened and four girls walked in. One of them looked at me and smiled as she passed our booth.

"Wow!" I said, nudging Jimmy. "Who's that?"

He turned and studied the girls as they sat down in a booth along the back wall. "You mean that brunette in the blue blouse?"

"Yeah," I said. "She smiled at me."

"She's a new girl. From Geneva, I think. I don't remember her name, but she's gonna be a freshman. Ain't she a beauty?"

July Sunset
poetry from Ron Bailey

the sun cools off this
afternoon, sucks
grape and cherry popsicles
drips them down her chin

harlot that she is
drags the tip of her steaming
tongue across the belly of the sky
time and time again,
tracing whisk broom trails,
purple and red,
toward the darkening day

i taste her vaporous
breath
in slow gasps

Creek
memoir from Linda McLean

I've walked along it so many times now that it calls to me. I can just see it from our back porch in the winter when the leaves are down, a sparkling ribbon meandering effortlessly. I am soothed by knowing it is there no matter the season.

Walks to the creek with my pooch Milo are especially joy-filled, no matter how many times we've tread the same path. Spring is my favorite time to wander, the trees still in bud, allowing spectacular wide-angle views that capture so much land and water and sky. The handsome white birches—sentinels of the land—beckon us further into the woods. Fiddle-head ferns begin their uncoiling near the creek that gushes and surges. The distant overhead honking makes my heart sing, continuing to refresh that sense of hope unique to spring.

Ah—but then there is summer, when the creek is truly accessible for wading and watching crawdads scatter while searching for treasures. We linger there, I to my knees and Milo swimming, filling our lungs with freshness, our sights brimming with such beauty that we can only thank God for the privilege. Milo enjoys cooling off as much as I do, his curly black fur clinging to his chicken-bone legs. My walking stick steadies me in the rushing flow as I pick my way along the rocky bottom.

I chat with Milo a lot on our walks, telling him stories of long-gone, beloved pooches who traveled these parts with me, and I am grateful the woods and creek rouse these happy memories. I sing to Milo, too: I love to go a-wandering...no embarrassment, for nature is my audience. Milo goes about his business, running and sniffing and exploring. He is happy to be with me on our journeys to the creek, taken through hallowed woods that are surely rife with their own memories of animal and human friends—the rocks, silent historians; the trees, respiring diarists.

Stone Throwers
fiction from Kirk House

Nobody missed him, and before long, everyone forgot his name. He'd joined the Continental Army for Sullivan's invasion of the Finger Lakes, burning the Iroquois towns, ruining their farms, cutting down their orchards, polluting their wells, and stealing or defiling their stores. But even in that hard army he was a hard, hard man, who glared far more than he spoke. Soldiers and officers alike both walked wide of him.

He didn't like them any more than they liked him. They sent him out on sentry duty one night as the army was pulling out, encamped for the night near the north end of Seneca Lake. He got to his assigned post all right, grunting at the man he replaced, but instead of standing guard he just kept walking into the nighttime forest, without any plans but bending generally southwestwards.

There was an unenthusiastic search in the morning, and brief speculation that he'd been killed by Indians. But since there were no signs of struggle he was quickly marked down as a deserter, with a relieved sense of good riddance, and the army hurried on eastward, and nobody missed him at all.

Two or three mornings later he stood in leafy cover by the east shore of Keuka Lake, opposite the tip of the Bluff, watching a Seneca couple and their young son make breakfast on the narrow beach. He wasn't much of a soldier, but he was something of a woodsman. He had kept his musket in good repair, and when he judged the moment had come he brought it up to his shoulder. His ball slammed deep into the back of the Seneca man; the shooter dropped his single-shot weapon and burst onto the little beach. The lake was still echoing his shot when he hatcheted the woman to the ground.

The boy, by then, was racing through the underbrush, but the head start didn't add much to his short life. Four minutes later the hatchet swung again, and again, and the deserter was annoyed, when he checked the boy, to see that he wore or carried nothing worth taking. Hiking back to the beach he found that the woman, though she would never wake again, still breathed, and put an end to that, then looted her body. The man was dead, and his possessions quickly pilfered. Finally the killer sat down to eat. That's why he'd waited before firing, until the woman had breakfast fully cooked.

Once he'd eaten every speck of their meal he decided to try the man's moccasins on, and threw them back into the man's face when they didn't fit. A little stone circle near the fire held a little tobacco heap. This puzzled him, for there seemed no purpose to it, and things he didn't understand (and they were many) disturbed him. He pocketed the tobacco, and kicked the stones apart, then kicked sand over the fire. He slapped at his neck as something stung—a wasp or a deerfly, maybe—but didn't catch whatever it was.

He combed through their things one last time, dumped his keepers into their canoe, and pushed himself off across Keuka's waters. Having a full stomach, he had no interest in the geese and ducks he passed along the way. Having an empty soul, he gave no glance to September's autumn leaves on the dramatic slopes.

Helped by a bit of a breeze he paddled angling across the lake and southwards, putting ashore on the West Side about where there would one day be a hamlet called Urbana. Since he wasn't planning to ever use the canoe again he kicked it in, so that nobody else would either. Then he shouldered his musket and set off southward on a long-established Indian footpath, with the lake on his left hand and the forest on his right, every step leaving the army, with its angry sergeants and demanding officers, farther behind. He'd joined because he liked breaking things and hurting people, and decided he might as well do it with sanction and pay, but all in all it hadn't been worth the aggravation.

He kept one slitted eye on the forest, because he kept getting the sense he heard movement in there.

An occasional plink or plunk in the ferns at his feet convinced him that rain was starting up. A stinging pain by his right ear got him swinging his hand to drive away the wasp, but he never found one. Then there were two thunks on his chest, making him look up. Hail? The day was dismal and overcast, but it didn't seem to be doing anything.

Shaking himself, he continued southward, but had only gone a couple of rods when another plink struck the tree trunk he was passing, and then his ear stung again. This time, though, he had marked the direction from which the tiny missiles came. With a roar, he charged into the underbrush.

Then came to a halt, and peered around. He was, for all he could tell, completely alone in the wood. No brush twitched. No figure crouched. No leaves rustled. But someone had been throwing, or shooting, at him.

Then something struck the back of his head, from the lake side. He roared and spun around, just in time to get hit in the chest, but this time he saw the object bounce, and caught it. When he opened his hand, he held a pebble on his palm. A pebble? Maybe someone had a crook or a sling, and that was why he hadn't spotted anyone? Were they farther off than he'd expected?

But to throw or shoot from that angle, his tormentor would have to be standing knee-deep in the Lake. And there was no one there.

Spitting into the lake, he headed south again, picking up the pace. Pebbles he could bear, and sooner or later someone would mis-step into sight, and then his hatchet would have some more fun.

A fair-sized rock struck his shoulder, numbing his upper arm.

Not being a man for campfire stories, or even for company, he'd never heard Iroquois tales of the Gahongas, knee-high people who haunted the forests and streams, and who excelled at throwing stones.

And at beating drums, and dancing to their drums.

Who looked out for people who showed them respect.

For instance, by leaving tobacco offerings.

And punished those who hurt those people.

The next rock took him in the gut, and he stumbled, and whooshed out breath, but kept on walking, and speeded up again.

Three times along his way he charged roaring into the woods, swinging his hatchet and screaming threats, and brushes and branches twitched, but he never saw a soul, and pebbles kept on flying, mixed more and more with bigger rocks.

He started to run, and the rocks got bigger yet.

When he staggered to a slower pace, the pebbles resumed, with a few larger rocks. Run and the rocks got bigger. Walk, and the pebbles flew.

He walked.

And stung.

And bled.

He crossed what would one day be called the Gulf Stream, then splashed through what would later be the Glen Brook, stumbled into the space that would one day be Hammondsport, and roared his pleasure, for there in a clearing was a huge granite boulder where he could take his stand. He shoved his back against the rock, screamed "Come on, then!" Not being much of a soldier, he hadn't bothered to reload his musket, but he gripped his hatchet in one hand and his bayonet in the other. If they wanted to get to him, they'd have to show themselves at last.

They didn't. A volley of pebbles the size of acorns pummelled him all over. Then a volley of rocks the size of chestnuts.

Then another volley of rocks, this time the size of duck's eggs, knocked him down to his knees. He tried to blink blood out of his eyes, and he strained to hear something, anything, through the drumbeats pounding right into his ears. He tried to push back up onto his feet, but this time each of the rocks was the size of a man's fist, and down he went face-first, still struggling and shaking himself.

A little.

Rocks as long as a canoe blade sailed from the brush and crashed all over him, and all around him, hiding him more and more from view. And more. And more. Until he was gone, his hatchet was gone, his musket was gone, all his stolen goods were gone. Covered in a heap of huge rocks, piled up against the huge granite boulder.

In time, briars and brambles covered the pile. When the first whites muscled in they loved the spot by the lake, but they didn't like the briars, or the pile of rocks. They didn't like it, and they avoided it, and they didn't often speak of it. It became a whispered legend, and old folks told tales of unhappy moans and unexplainable frights they'd had when they'd passed those rocks at night. But some of the old folks said they'd found the rocks near the mouth of the Inlet. And others said it was by the Gulf Stream. A few swore that they'd come across it in the Glen, and one even insisted it was half-way up the Winding Stair.

At least people *knew* about the rocks. As for Sullivan's deserter, it hadn't taken long for every human being on earth to forget that he'd ever encumbered the ground.

And nobody missed him.

Abandoned Barn
poetry from Gary Snook

What ghosts
Do you hold
What tales
Would you tell
If you could
Only speak
Or do you speak
On windy nights
Is that your voice
We hear
With every tug
And pull
Of the wind
Is the groaning
Of timbers
And shriek
Of rusty nails
Your voice
Telling us
Listen to me now
I speak to you
Of the things
I have seen
In a hundred years
And more

I speak to you
Of a lifetime
Of sweat and toil
And blood given up

Of children
Who laughed
And played
 Before me
On long ago
 Summer days
Of love found
And lost again
Of lives lived
And in the end
Their return
 To the earth
Just as I return
Bit by bit
Slowly settling
A little more
Into the soil
With every
Weathering day

Muck
fiction from Bethany Snyder

Olive was on her way to deliver tomatoes and jam to her sister-in-law Ada when the accident happened. Muff had moved the family to a farm out on West Swamp Road in the late 1980s, and even though Olive had been there hundreds of times, she often mistakenly turned onto East Swamp Road instead, which she had done again today.

She realized her error when she saw the sign for East Muck Road—which of course did not intersect with West Swamp Road (although, to be fair, neither did West Muck Road)—and when she tapped the brakes, the jar of jam flew off and then rolled under the seat.

Olive reached for it at the same time as she was slowing down to use the intersection with Muck to course correct. There were no other cars around, which wasn't unusual for a Monday morning just after sunrise, though she'd heard the distant clamor of farm machinery through the open window as she'd driven up and out of town. Of course, it was harder to hear a horse and buggy, and Olive saw it at the last possible moment. Still bent forward with her hand under the passenger seat, fingers slipping on quilted glass, she yanked the steering wheel hard to the left, sending the car sliding across the gravel shoulder on the wrong side of the road, rocks pinging off the undercarriage, and thumping over the grassy ditch.

She used both feet to press the brake, and the impact of her forehead and cheek on the dashboard was so painful and disorienting that she didn't realize she'd broken several of her fingers until a pair of rough, sun-darkened hands were pulling at her blouse, trying to help her from the car. She yelped in pain.

"Ma'am? Are you all right?"

The car had stopped in—and was sinking into—an especially wet spot in the field. The pant legs of the young Mennonite man trying to help Olive were dark with mud and manure.

"Oh, I'm fine," she said, offering him a weak smile. He took her gently under her left elbow and lifted her up and out of the car. Her sandaled feet squished in the cool mud and pooling water. She held her broken hand as close to her body as she dared. "Well, not completely fine."

"Your eye," the young man said, offering her a clean white handkerchief. Olive pressed it to her face, and it came away soaked with dark red blossoms of warm blood.

The man pointed at her handbag, on the seat next to the basket of tomatoes. "Do you have a telephone?" Olive shook her head. "I'll send my son for help and wait with you," the man said. She slumped against him gratefully.

In the time it took for the young man to get to town and alert the police, Olive had fallen asleep with her chin on her chest, her bottom on the undamaged passenger side of the sun-warmed hood of the car. She woke to the wail of the ambulance siren, the raised voices of men calling to each other, the crackle of a police radio. Three blond children in cotton bonnets and straw hats, squatting in the long grass at the side of the road with their chins in their hands, kept a close watch.

Ada caught a ride to town with Jimmy Hopkins two days later, and the sisters-in-law shared afternoon coffee and Ada's blue-ribbon pecan kringle on Olive's screened-in back porch, Olive's splinted and taped fingers propped on a pillow on the arm of her rocking chair. Waves lapped at the sagging boards of the old dock. A breeze that hinted of autumn ruffled the paper napkins on the little table between them. The gratitude Olive had felt when she saw Ada climb out of Jimmy's truck carrying her overnight bag made her feel as if her chest would crack apart.

When Muff first started courting Ada, Olive had already moved out of the big house on Clinton Street and into the cozy cottage on the lower lake road. She spent the summer changing the paint from bleached gray to a cheery yellow, raking seaweed off the little crescent beach, and planting bunches of pink and white impatiens in the window boxes her brother had made her as a housewarming gift. He brought Ada around one Saturday night in the hottest part of August, and they'd made a fire down by the water and gotten drunk on Aunt Aggie's elderberry wine. Olive and Ada shared Olive's narrow bed that night—even with Mother and Father four miles away in town and with his clunky class ring on a gold chain around Ada's neck, Muff didn't dare make room for her next to him in the nest of blankets on the porch floor—the backs of their knees slick with sweat. As an old woman, Olive could still remember the smoky smell of the hair at the nape of Ada's neck.

Of course there had been speculation about Olive's sexuality from as far back as high school, when she kept her dark curls short and was the only girl in her class to go to stag to the junior prom. When she came back from college with a degree and without a husband, tongues clucked, and when she bought the cottage on her own, jaws wagged so feverishly she expected to be featured on the front page of paper.

She'd loved Ada from the moment they'd met, Ada in a pair of blue checkered pedal pushers, her thick blonde hair pulled into a high ponytail, clutching a basket filled with homemade molasses cookies, but she had never been *in* love with her—or anyone, for that matter. Olive counted Ava among the very few interesting people she'd met over the course of her life, and although she thought of the half dozen or so of them with affection, none of them made her heart race or her stomach cramp or whatever other physical sensation one was supposed to experience in the presence of romantic love.

"Does it hurt?" Ada asked, nodding at Olive's fingers. Her feet on the ottoman were swollen, her ankles straining the straps of her orthopedic sandals.

"Not too much," Olive replied.

"Good." Ada rested her hands on the curve of her belly, rubbed at her wedding ring with her thumb. "Imagine it's hard to do things, being right-handed." Ada was ambidextrous.

Olive raised an eyebrow. "What are you getting at, Ada Jean?"

She exhaled, leaning over the arm of her rocker, her breath thick with coffee and pastry. "I'm getting at that if you were waiting for a sign to sell this place, you just got one." Olive stiffened and moved her broken fingers out of Ada's reach. "I have plenty of room just going to waste. I'll brush your hair and help you button your blouse. Come live with me."

"I can button my own blouse."

"Can you?" Ada pointed at the bottom of Olive's shirt, the right side lower than the left, an empty buttonhole gaping there. She giggled, but Olive got out of her chair with a grunt and snatched the kringle from the table. "Come back, I'm just picking!"

The kitchen was her favorite part of the cottage, with its little window looking out over the scrap of yard to the Griffins' place next door and the dark blue expanse of the lake beyond. Her parents had thought she was ridiculous to buy such a tiny house, sure that she would change her mind about a husband and children one day, and need space for a brood to play and grow. But she'd fallen hard for the white-washed walls, the hand-carved ladder leading up to the loft bedroom, the built-in shelves in the living room, perfect for her ever-expanding collection of books. People were hard to love, but places and things were not.

It was true that it was a good time—maybe the best time in what was left of Olive's life—to sell. The housing market had never been so hot, or so the young man had told her just the week before, as he sat across from her at the kitchen table, his coffee grown cold and slice of pumpkin pie reduced to crumbs, picking at a chip in the formica. Olive took the estimate he offered, folded it and tucked it into the pocket of her apron, shooing him to the door with a promise to think about it. She'd lain awake long into the night in the same bed she'd shared with Ada when they were new friends, thinking about the enormity of the number the young man had scratched onto the back of his business card. The thought of someone bulldozing her home and erecting a monstrous mansion in its stead made her clutch the covers until her forearms ached.

Olive pulled the tin foil from the drawer next to the stove. Before she wrapped up the remains of Ada's dessert, she cut herself another slice. Chewing was a challenge, what with her jaw set so tight. She swallowed hard, the pastry a thick lump in her throat.

After a while, Ada brought in the coffee cups and napkins, and they made up while doing the dishes, Olive washing and Ada drying and putting away. It was a squeeze for both of them to work in the cramped kitchen, what with Olive's grandmother's butcher block taking up half the space. Ada loved to say she had permanent bruising on her hips from running into the blasted thing. Olive could no longer crawl beneath it to see the initials she and Muff had carved there when they were young, but sometimes she bent to trace the unseen letters with her fingertips.

When clean-up was done, Ada bustled Olive out to the hammock while she worked on dinner—boiling potatoes, shelling peas, squeezing lemon into the sun tea that had been brewing on the picnic table. Olive's contribution to the meal was the remnants of a box of fried chicken from Seneca Farms she'd bought the day before.

She read for a bit, and then dozed to the hum of motorboats

running up and down the length of the lake, the yelp of youthful voices, the distant drone of a lawn mower. When she woke, the sun had slipped close to the top of the bluff.

"Ada?"

The Griffins' dog yipped at her from its perch in the back window. She struggled to sit, swinging her legs over the side of the canvas, feeling for the grass with her bare feet. A corner of her book, a mystery novel she'd picked up at the library book sale, dug into her thigh.

"Help an old girl, come on," she called, but only the puppy replied.

Olive tried hoisting herself out by grabbing at the rope that connected the hammock to the tree, but her left hand was too weak. The hammock began to rock. She tried to stop the motion with her feet, but instead she managed to push off against the ground, the hammock now swinging wildly. With a grimace, she tucked her broken hand close and, on the downswing, pulled her legs in and rolled out of the hammock, tumbling onto the sparse grass with a yelp.

When Muff was in kindergarten, Father had taken Mother to Herr Jensen's for their anniversary, leaving ten-year-old Olive in charge. She'd boiled hot dogs and heated a can of beans for dinner, made Muff drink all his milk. After, Muff asked if he could go out to play, and she'd made sure he knew to come back in when the little hand on his watch was on the seven and the big hand on the six.

Her cousin Robin called just as she was finishing sweeping the kitchen, and—the promise of uninterrupted phone time too delicious to deny—it was nearly full dark by the time Olive realized Muff hadn't come back inside.

As she made her way to the back door of her cottage, rubbing at the sore spot on her hip from where she'd hit the ground tumbling out of the hammock, Olive remembered the way the panic had tightened her throat that long-ago night, how the armpits of her favorite plaid dress had grown damp with sweat as she crashed out into the night, shouting her brother's name. She resisted the urge to call again for Ada, afraid to hear the fear in her voice.

Muff had been found playing jacks under the streetlight in front of a friend's house down on Stark Avenue. Olive had swatted his bottom the whole way back up to the house, both of them crying. She apologized with a cookie snuck from the blue tin in the back of the cupboard by the sink—making him brush his teeth an extra minute so Mother wouldn't smell the sweet crumbs on his breath when she came in to kiss him goodnight—and he pinky promised to never leave the yard again, as long as he lived, with a crossed heart thrown in for good measure.

Olive let the screen door slam, but there was no sound from inside the cottage. Peeled potatoes were cooling in the colander in the sink, and the table had been set, a mason jar of garden cukes swimming in vinegar and sugar as the centerpiece. She peered down the hall, but the bathroom door was open, the nightlight she left plugged in throwing a rectangle of pale yellow across the carpet runner.

She stood still and closed her eyes. The refrigerator kicked off. A fly buzzed at the screen over the sink. Then, faintly, she heard Ada's snore, coming from above.

It had seemed impossible to climb the old ladder to the loft with only one working hand, which is why Olive had been sleeping in the living room, but she managed better than she expected. The loft was the first reason Ada had offered for selling the cottage—no eighty-two-year-old woman in her right mind should want to climb up and down a ladder several times a night to relieve her bladder. Olive had replied that she could get a bed pan, or a fireman's pole.

Ada was curled up on Olive's bed with her face to the wall. When Olive lowered herself onto the mattress, Ada rolled toward her. Her eyes were red and puffy.

"What's wrong?"

"I was looking in the pantry for an onion, and then I remembered you keep them in the drawer in the fridge, and when I opened it I saw the radishes and—"

Ada flapped her hand and then let it fall to the quilt. Olive gave it a squeeze.

"And it reminded me Muff, of course, you remember how he'd eat them straight out of the garden, still covered in dirt?" Olive nodded. "I know it's been two years and I shouldn't be so tender still, but I miss him so much, it feels like someone took my heart out and laid it on the table."

Olive laughed. Ada stared, the corners of her mouth turned down. "You know what I mean." She clucked her tongue. "Or you don't, I guess. You know—" Ada struggled to sit up, the hem of her shorts riding up so that Olive caught sight of the bottom of the scar from her hip replacement, a faded old zipper— "I always felt sorry for you, no one for you to love and no one to love you back."

It was a familiar fight, and Olive let the old anger flow over her, tightening her shoulders. She felt Ada seething beside her, heard the sharp intake of breath over her clenched teeth. "Well, I do love you," she said instead, and the air in the room softened. Ada's head found its way to Olive's shoulder, and they sat in silence until shadows filled the room and someone's stomach growled at the thought of cold chicken and warm potato salad.

Olive climbed down first, and as she held up her good hand to catch her sister-in-law if she fell, she startled both of them by saying, "It's been three years, not two."

Jimmy Hopkins came by after breakfast, the back of his truck loaded down with old window frames, stuttered with broken glass like sharp teeth. It had rained hard in the night, and the postage stamp of Olive's front yard was a mucky mess. She stood on the bottom step leading up to the house, the cement cool and damp under her bare feet.

Ada waved as Jimmy drove away, one hand clutching her overnight bag. Olive had promised to come stay for a week on West Swamp Road as soon as her car was back from Marbles, to see how she liked living in the country, waking up to birdsong and the rustling of deer in the trees instead of the rhythm of waves on the shore, the insect buzz of a seaplane high overhead. Ada promised peach pie and pot roast, back scratches and control of the television remote, euchre with Susan and Sharon from next door after fish fry takeout on Friday night.

As Olive wrapped her cast in a plastic bag so she could shower, tearing the duct tape with her teeth, she wondered at the empty places a person left after fifty-six years. She imagined the sunken spot in the bed where Muff had slept, the worn places at the dining room table where his elbows had rested as he said grace, the winter boots at the back of the hall closet, gloves still tucked inside. She pictured Ada alone in that big farmhouse kitchen, holding her beating heart in her cupped hands.

Olive's bad shoulder ached, and she rubbed at the loose skin above her collarbone. She'd need a nap in the afternoon, though she would avoid the hammock until her fingers were healed. They'd gone to bed late the night before, skin marbled with gooseflesh after an impromptu skinny dip under the moonless sky, Olive's injured hand bobbing out of the water like a tiny buoy. They'd giggled their way up the grass, holding their bathrobes close around their throats, watching for lights to come on at the Griffins'.

She poured herself the rest of the sun tea and carried the orange bowl full of chicken bones outside. Three white sailboats turned the corner from the west branch, headed north. The sky was heavy and close, but a stiff wind dried the damp curls at the back of Olive's neck. She turned back and looked at her little cottage, a spot of sunshine in the gray, and thought again about that young man's business card, tacked to the wall inside next to the telephone. She picked up the bowl and flung the bones across the wet grass. Something would come in the night and take them away, grateful for the gift. Olive sat and watched the sailboats grow smaller and smaller until her vision blurred, and then she turned her back and went inside.

Ever Green
poetry from Carolyn Clark

Each ornament
adorns
remembrances,
sparks recognition,
delights.

Concolor from Oregon seed
wintered here some eleven years,
according to its cut stump,
post-drought.

Laughing, we snap pics of our find:
Geoff with bow-saw in this teeth,
me leaning like an elf, again
in Mark's forest: *Fir Farm*

where the trees run free
above and below deep ruts
his tractor keeps tracking
back and forth, over the years

where bluebirds perch,
ragweed is queen
and the wild things *are...*
ever green.

—for Mark

A Change of Diet
poetry from Carol Mikoda

For many years I walked in the woods to survive,
each day seeking leaf-filtered light, the solid
company of trees and stars, scurrying rodents
in the underbrush, whistle of winter wind in bare
branches, as food for my soul. Now I wonder
how I lasted so long without being near water
at least once a day, surveying the acreage
as it falls under the vault, spreading beneath sun,
moon, clouds. My new companions are billowing
wave, occasional whitecap, and stretch of sky
where clarity reigns or one or few or black clouds
float, or soft fog accompanies rain
or snowfall. Haunting nuanced blues and grays
replace muted greens and rich browns;
the horizon sometimes a sharp line, sometimes
a mere misty suggestion of Avalon or Brigadoon
as I gaze. On calm days, a mirror spreads
from shore to shore, east to west, offering
two skies as options: reality above, or maybe
laid out like a glassy tablecloth or television screen,
into which I can jump, holding hands with Alice.
Or I can chase a White Rabbit from the deck
of a boat where each gust and surge vibrates
in my core: I brace myself to stay upright.

The Importance of Place
memoir from Laurie Weller

I do not like to fly. I firmly believe that the phenomenon of mechanical flight exists on the fringe of what the universe will comfortably allow. In spite of numerous explanations of thrust, drag, weight and lift, I cannot board even the shortest flight without an underlying fear of unkind retribution. I've seen what can happen when God's creatures try to fool Mother Nature, so I avoid airplanes whenever I can get away with it.

I don't like to fly, but it was Valentine's Day. Snow was in the forecast and avoidance was not an option; I had to catch the earliest plane north. I got to the airport ahead of time, hoping to go standby to Ottawa, where my husband was waiting. He was on assignment there, and I was way down in Northern Virginia. It's a ten-hour drive from there to the Canadian border, up through the mountains of Pennsylvania and the center of my native, beloved New York state. In February, the choice as to mode of transportation was clear, and I was resigned; I would fly to be with my love.

After conferring with the staff at the gate, I parked myself in the waiting area and attempted to distract myself by thinking about the writing assignment I'd been given earlier in the week. I was taking a course entitled *The Importance of Place*, and our task was to "tell a nature story." Now, I am about as far from being a child of nature as one can possibly get, and I was feeling a bit stymied. My version of a hike involves walking from the front door to my parked car, and I've been known to kill a cactus. Not on purpose, of course; actually, I think it might have voluntarily checked out rather than face a dubious future with me. Perhaps I could write about that—POV the cactus.

Before long, I heard the news that I had scored a seat on a 4:45 pm flight. Trudging across the tarmac to the diminutive, waiting jet, I told myself that I'd be in Canada in a scant one hour and fifteen minutes. "I can endure just about anything for an hour," I thought as I teetered up the narrow stairs and found my way to my window seat. Armed with a bag of M&Ms and a good book, I was strapped and trapped in a metal tube with fifty total strangers, hurtling down the runway and headed toward the sky. "Only an hour, only an hour," I chanted in my head as we ascended through the clouds. The window shade was open, so I covered the left side of my face with my hand, trying to pretend I was on the couch in my living room. Rays of pink-tinged light filtered through my fingers, touching my cheek and tempting me to take a look outside. I took a gulp of the Diet Coke provided by the stewardess, wishing it was fortified with Bacardi, and ventured a glance through the window.

The sky was clear and clean, the horizon etched by the slowly setting sun. The snow-covered ground below was anonymous, crisscrossed by nameless roads and fences, and I didn't know where in the world I was. Suspended in mid-air, held aloft by forces that I did not understand or trust, the landscape floated along under me. "Almost there, almost there," said my mind. And then, in a moment of sheer serendipity, my eye caught the shape of something familiar. Almost before I understood what I was seeing, I gasped. Out loud. Below, looking up at me with the face of a familiar old friend, was the y-shaped outline of Keuka Lake. Next to it was the long, narrow slate-gray form of Seneca and, though I could not see it from my seat on the opposite side of the plane, I knew that my cherished Owasco was peacefully shining in the soft, diminishing light. "Oh, man," I breathed. Nose firmly pressed to the window, I tried to hold onto the sight for as long as I could; couch or no couch, I was home. In the glow of twilight, twinkling lights were flickering on in all the living rooms below me, and I beheld my nature story. Right there, beneath my soaring feet, was the never-ending gift of place, of nature and nurture combined. It had never felt more important and, just for a moment, I forgot that I don't like to fly.

Monica's Pies
or An Ordinary Day Not So Long Ago
nonfiction from Karen Lee Hones

Somebody asked me, what's the secret to your mother's long life? Without giving it much thought, I said prayer, hair (neat but not fussy), and dessert.

Mother lived in small towns in Michigan until age eighty, when I had the brilliant idea to bring her and Father to San Francisco. They moved into a remodeled unit on the ground floor of the Mission District building where I also lived. (I never thought I'd have to live in an apartment, Mother said when they arrived.) Father died a month later. Mother lasted six years in the City, but never liked living alone. My youngest sister Marge then convinced her to move to Rochester to live with her and my niece Frankie in a house right across from a Catholic church.

I love visiting them. For one thing, we don't have seasonal changes in San Francisco. More importantly, when Mother was on my turf I was more easily pulled down into her grief and dissatisfaction. Here, as frequent visitor, I can savor daily pleasures like a tourist while sharing the responsibility for Mother's care.

This Sunday morning at Marge's I wake up early and watch the pale light out front make the leaves from the old maple shimmer. I walk to Bagel Land to pick up everything bagels and a New York Times before Mass.

When I get home, Mother has dressed in neatly creased beige pants and a purple sweater. Her new short haircut makes her look artistic and soignée. Mother had been a Latin teacher until she married at 25 and then raised eleven children. All during my childhood she'd get a cut and perm at Mrs. Wolf's Beauty Salon in East Ann Arbor a few times a year. She sometimes wore lipstick, but otherwise didn't bother with make-up. She cared about how she looked, though, and even in her 90's would comment, that's a good one or that's terrible, when I'd show her a photo I'd taken of her on my phone.

I'm wearing my uniform of black turtleneck and jeans. Frankie, who will push the wheelchair across the street, has on what Mother calls a darling dress. Our disparate trio makes its way across half an hour before the start of the service as Mother likes to be early. Frankie parks the wheelchair next to the first pew and Mother buries her nose in the bulletin. I sit and meditate. As people trickle in, they approach Mother and say hi. These are her people now. I think she is so lucky to have found a new community in her nineties.

During the church service, Mother sits with an absorbed look on her face, but she's hard of hearing, and can only follow because she's been to Mass a million times before.

Afterward, Frankie pushes her back across the street, and Mother sits in her chair and finishes reading the bulletin. The school children will be selling sloppy Joes this week, she says. And, there's a memorial mass for Joan Lemming. She adds, I hadn't realized she died.

I wonder which Joan that is. Mother told me there are so many Joans in Rochester that they have a Joan luncheon from time to time and as many as seventy Joans show up.

I say would you like a BLT for lunch and she says that sounds wonderful. Mother loves the way I cook bacon in the oven. I generously salt tomatoes from Wegmans to enhance their flavor. Frankie toasts sourdough and helps me assemble the sandwiches.

Marge arrives home from her noodle workout in the swimming

pool. She asks, would anyone like to go for a ride in the country? Would we! Going for a ride is probably Mother's favorite thing, after daily Mass. At the end of their time in Michigan, she would coax Father into the car, and drive him out to the rural areas where there were still barns and open fields, trees and crops. Tooling along the back roads was their meditation, I often thought.

Mother changes into comfortable sweats for the ride and Frankie helps her into the front passenger seat. Of all of us, it's Mother's granddaughter Frankie who is naturally the most solicitous and affectionate. Grandma, can I comb your hair? Do you need a sweater? Guess what? I think we should see how many words we can make using the letters in the word Canandaigua. I'll start. D-u-n-g, dung. Your turn. I-g-u-a-n-a, iguana, Mother fires back.

A nondriver, I settle into the back seat with Frankie and sink into an uncharacteristic passivity. I ride buses and trains and I fly, but cars are a world within which I have little or no agency. Marge is a good driver (though I notice she's gotten more aggressive since the divorce). As we leave behind familiar Rochester neighborhoods, I look out the window and daydream.

So many trees. Coming from parched California, I am always amazed at the lush greenery of the Rochester area. I love the frequent rains. On this autumn day, though, it's not raining. The pale light gives the rich colors of the falling leaves a surprise elegance.

The ride isn't hilly but the landscape is rolling, voluptuous, feminine. We pass through Victor where Marge and I have recently been shopping for furniture. Marge is mulling over a loveseat we saw in a consignment store that would fit well in Mother's study.

Although I notice a Wendy's or an Office Depot here and there along the route, the little towns we pass through have an intimate, particular character—so different from the iconic skyline of home, but charming and calming.

When I see the sign for Naples, I say oh, hey, Marge, are we going to Monica's Pies? And she says yep. Her good friend, Leslie, a teacher at the high school, works part-time at Monica's. I adore Leslie. She singlehandedly catered my mother's 95th birthday party. My sibs still talk about the pulled pork sliders, and luscious cupcakes—not to mention her sangfroid in the kitchen, serving over a hundred of us—family and random close friends from all over.

Marge pulls into the space in front of Monica's Pies. I say Mother, do you want to get out and stretch your legs.

I think I'll stay in the car, she says.

She's gotten old. In the past she would always want to get out. But now, I think she worries about having to use the bathroom, maybe falling—even though we have the walker in the trunk. So I stay with her, and Frankie and Marge go in to get a pie. They return with two, apple and grape.

On the ride home Frankie is a little peckish, but I know Mother is too tired to leave the car. I remind them that last night I made the chicken with biscuits (Bisquick!) that Mother likes—and we can have that before we dig in to the pie.

Marge pushes quickly through a deserted intersection. I tap her on the shoulder and say can we stop somewhere to get vanilla ice cream so we can have pie a la mode a la Jack Kerouac to celebrate our road trip? Mother says, that sounds good. I smile and lean back.

Frankie pipes up, Grandma, I spy with my little eye...

If Perry City Sounds Too Grand
poetry from Daphne Solá

it's a misnomer if ever there was one.
Perry, as the natives call it,
is a very small place
but can truly claim
that in the nineteenth century
a railroad planned to stop here
. . .a promise never fulfilled.

We arrived from a great
metropolis
so wet behind the ears
it does not bear thinking on,
two city-dwellers plunked down among
several hundred farmers and country-folk

and *folk* is too cute a word by far
to honor their accumulated
wisdom and knowledge.

Language, used sparsely,
and full of unembarrassed silences was
also full of dry humor.
Been to the auction again, Bob?
only required a quick eye
to the bed of a neighbor's pickup truck,
which newly contained a rusted harrow
and a set of antique . . . but usable tools.

Where we struggled at times

to shake off our city ways
our children grew up country,
absorbing through the skin
an upstate way of doing things
as well as an upstate dialect.
They ran barefoot almost half the year,
picked violets in the lawn,
knew the best sites for wild strawberries,
and dropped from a willow-hung rope
into a pool of water known as the Depot, a
linguistic variation on
The Deep Hole.

They could fearlessly chase home a fairly
aggressive fellow,
Homer the Goose, running him up the
road with a long stick to the neighbor's
house, knowing he only came down to
visit when he was lonesome.

Most improbably, and it remains a favorite
memory, in a fiercely cold winter our
children learned to ice-skate in a woods
that in summer had standing water.
They whizzed through and around the
trees
and forever after thought that skating
in a set round space
was very dull indeed.

About the Authors

ALEX ANDRASIK is a librarian and proud geek from Fredonia, New York, who currently resides in Penn Yan. You should follow his writing and activist work: the LGBTQ+ social group Keuka Compass, the immigration-focused Penn Yan Action Coalition, the Finger Lakes Justice Partnership, and his political and cultural work at the Brackish Line. All can be found on Facebook, for a start.

RON BAILEY lives in Penfield, New York, and has a small place on Canandaigua Lake, where he does most of his writing. As a kid, he grew up in Syracuse in a "not-at-all-well-to-do" family, and a trip to Uncle Ted's place on Keuka Lake was summer vacation. He has had poetry published in *The Red Wheelbarrow*, *Hazmat*, and *Black Creek Review*, and a short piece of humorous prose in *The New York Times*.

JOHN BUCHHOLZ was born in Penn Yan, raised in Lyons, and currently lives near Greene, New York. He's a Cornell alumnus and is retired from a labor relations career in Philadelphia. His most recent writing has appeared in *Byline, Reminisce, Down Memory Lane,* and *Bluff & Vine*.

CAROLYN CLARK, Ph.D., is a devoted teacher and a personal trainer. Indebted to teachers at Cornell University, Brown University, and The Johns Hopkins University for degrees in Classics-related fields, she enjoys riding, writing woodlands lyric poetry, and finding mythology everywhere.

LAURA DENNIS teaches at a small college in Kentucky. She edits the Attachment & Trauma Network blog and co-edits book reviews for *Mom Egg Review*. Her creative nonfiction has been recognized in two writing contests and has been published in *MER Vox Quarterly, Bethlehem Writers Roundtable,* and *Change Seven*.

CATHY FRASER is a self-taught photographer born in Rochester, NY. She is primarily a portrait photographer, though she also does landscape and night photography. She has had her work shown in the Arts Center of Yates County and Image City Photography Gallery in Rochester. She is a full time resident of Penn Yan, NY.

ADELE GARDNER (gardnercastle.com) has had more than 350 poems published, and has a poetry book, *Halloween Hearts*, forthcoming in October 2022. Deep family connections to Keuka include Adele's first seven years in Keuka Park and Penn Yan; annual family reunions at Keuka Lake; and father Delbert, professor, and mother Marilyn, alumna, Keuka College.

JAMES HARLEY HANCOCK and his wife of 54 years, Patricia Lee Kykendall, have been living on Seneca Lake year-round these past 18 years. James taught in the Department of English/Philosophy, Monroe Community College, for 39 years, retiring in 2005. His avocation is reading and writing poetry and philosophy.

DEWEY HILL is a retired English teacher from the Albany, New York, public schools. He writes poetry, fishes, travels, and writes a few of his poems as songs for his baritone ukulele.

FRANK D. HILL is a freelance writer and (happily) former attorney and mediator who lives with his wife and daughter in Illinois. His poetry has appeared or is forthcoming in *Communion Arts Journal*, as part of the online exhibit Dream Geographies, and the online literary magazine, *Unfortunately,*.

BECKY HOLDER is a storyteller, writer, and teacher, currently living in Saratoga County, New York. Her family moved a lot (eleven times before she was ten), but finally found Keuka Lake, which has been her home ever since, no matter where she lives.

KAREN LEE HONES, a poet living in San Francisco, has spent a lot of time in Rochester and the Finger Lakes, where she has family and helped with her mother's care in the last years of her life. She has been published in journals such as the *Santa Clara Review*, *Prosodia*, *New Letters*, and *Yellow Silk*. Her poem "Dementia Pugilistica" will be published by *The MacGuffin* as the second runner up in its annual Poet Hunt.

MARLANA KAIN has been swimming in Conesus Lake for 59 summers. Raised in Williamsville, she worked in government affairs in DC after graduating from Purdue, then raised three children as a stay-at-home mom with her husband. Favorite things about the Finger Lakes? Simple pleasures, natural beauty, friendly people, and all the wine!

JUN LIU was born and raised in China, has studied and traveled in Germany, and is currently working and gardening in Canandaigua and Naples, New York. Her poems are often inspired by nature and seasonal changes that link with every aspect and depth of life.

AGNES MCCLEAR was born near Detroit, moved to Rochester in 1999, and worked in education until retirement. She now works part time at her local library and writes poetry and fiction. Agnes has published in *The Journal of General Internal Medicine* and written feature articles for newspapers in Michigan and Minnesota.

LINDA MCLEAN has lived in the Fingers Lake region for 15 years now. She takes her writing inspiration from hiking the area's limitless trails, where ideas for stories present themselves.

CAROL MIKODA lived in the Southern Tier of New York, just east of Binghamton, for many years. As COVID was closing everything down in 2020, she fell in love and moved to Hector. Her writing has been enriched by her proximity to Seneca Lake. Heer work has appeared in *Capsule Stories, Anatolios Magazine, New Feathers Anthology, Grief Becomes You,* and *Acta Victoriana.*

JOAN MISTRETTA grew up in Brooklyn and began writing poetry for her high school literary magazine. Being mostly retired from substance abuse counseling, she is active in St. Mark's Episcopal Church, League of Women Voters, and Southern Tier Interfaith Council. She has four great grandchildren.

ROGER PAGE is sixty-six years old and lives in Addison, New York, with his wife of forty years, Karen. In semi-retirement, he caters to an affection beyond measure for hounds, hunting, fishing, and writing about it. He is frequently published in outdoor magazines, and you can find a growing inventory of his self-published books on Amazon.

BARD PRENTISS is a professor emeritus from SUNY Cortland's Art Department. He is new to formal writing, having published three short natural history articles in *Life in the Finger Lakes* and one in *Wooden Canoe Journal* on paddling.

CHRISTINE PYANOE is a retired French and Spanish teacher who moved here after spending many summers on Keuka Lake. She owns Aubergine Bed and Breakfast in Penn Yan, and continues to be inspired every day by the beauty of the Finger Lakes.

RUTH ANNE (SMYTH) REAGAN was born in Addison, New York, graduated from Corning Northside High School, graduated from Syracuse University in 1951, and was hired as a music teacher in Marcellus. She married Bernard Reagan of Marcellus, and was active and in the fields of music, art and writing, as well as raising eight amazing children.

ELLEN HIRNING SCHMIDT's poems are in *Passager*, *The Avocet*, *Poetry Quarterly*, *Caesura*, *Connecticut River Review*, *Blood & Thunder*, *The Healing Muse*. She's a 2021 Connecticut Poetry Society prize winner. *Oh, say did you know* received the Helen Kay Chapbook Prize. She leads workshops in Ithaca, at Cornell, and Star Island, New Hampshire.

NONNA SHTIPELMAN grew up in Rochester, and spent almost twenty years working with brown bears, middle school students, and maximum security inmates in Alaska. She now lives in Fairport with her husband, Doug, who keeps her grounded, and their dog, Fast Eddie, who reminds them both to play in the snow.

LUCAS SMITH has lived in the Finger Lakes region for the past six years. He is an elementary teacher and lives with his wife, two cats, and dog in Shortsville. He writes poems, stories, and essays on his blog, oldcrowlibrary.blogspot.com.

GARY SNOOK has lived in the Finger Lakes region his entire life. He grew up in Waterloo and now has a home a short distance from Keuka Lake. The flora and fauna of the region has in the past inspired him, and is to this day an ongoing influence.

BETHANY SNYDER loves the sea, semi-colons, and superheroes. She has been voted best local/published author in the *Best of Rochester* poll four times. A native of Penn Yan, she earned a degree in creative writing from Bradford College in Massachusetts.

DAPHNE SOLÁ lives in the country near Ithaca, New York. She and her husband moved to Perry City many years ago, and never stop being grateful for their country setting. Solá is a pianist and printmaker, and owns an art gallery. Her prints and paper artwork have been shown in New York, Copenhagen, Denmark, Kyoto, Japan and Lima, Peru.

SARAH (PINNEO) TALLEy grew up on her family's vineyard in Penn Yan with a view of Keuka Lake. She is a physical therapist and lives with her husband and their dog in Raleigh, North Carolina. Her guilty pleasures include running, yoga, travel, adventures with friends, and assorted creative pursuits.

LAURIE WELLER grew up in Owego, New York, and has been coming to Owasco Lake since she spent the summer in Indian Cove with her best friend when she was 13. Her love for this unique and beautiful area has stayed with her and, when it came time for her husband and her to retire from the Washington, DC area, they came home at last and have never looked back.

SALLY WHITE grew up in the Southern Tier, but spent her adult life in Colorado. Her career as a botanist/ecologist, museum curator, and born-again historian led to writing nonfiction, especially nature essays. Though she's missing magpies and crispy potato chips, she's enjoying renewed life in New York.

About the Artist

CATHY Fraser is a self-taught photographer. Born in Rochester, New York, she is primarily a portrait photographer, and also dabbles in landscape and night photography. Her work has been shown in the Arts Center of Yates County and Image City Photography Gallery in Rochester. She is a full time resident of Penn Yan, New York.

Made in United States
North Haven, CT
08 November 2021